## PRAISE FOR ALLAN MASON

'A must-read for anyone in business. Allan gives you specific information to help you grow and properly manage your business, while minimising tax. It is packed with actionable advice and a dash of important mindset and human psychology principles. There is definitely something for every business owner in this book, no matter your level of success' **Pat Mesiti, Author**

'All the information I wish I'd had when I first started my business. It has solid business, money and tax advice that anyone in business should follow. Allan dives deep into key principles that will help you manage your business's cash flow and avoid overpaying taxes. Allan also openly discusses the emotional cost of running a business, which is often a hidden secret among many business owners, and how to avoid the trap of near-debilitating anxiety, which often comes with success. Read this book cover to cover – you'll be glad you did' **Steven Essa, Author**

'Essential reading for those seeking a magic formula for success that works every time or those who want to make more money and know how to keep it (by paying less tax). Allan Mason draws on experience from over 40 years as an accountant in practice and in business. As an entrepreneur, you must invest in yourself, be self-motivated to be successful in life and business, and have a growth mindset. Learning from people who have experience, knowledge and good judgement is paramount. By acting on and implementing what Allan has provided for you in this book, you will create more wealth and manage your business better, so you make more profit (and keep it). Plus, it will help you become wealthier and healthier, both emotionally and psychologically' **Lisa Fogarty, Founder, Performance Circle**

## ABOUT THE AUTHOR

**Allan Mason** is a chartered accountant, registered tax agent, registered company auditor, SMSF auditor and business advisor. He consults to many leading accounting firms and is a keynote speaker on tax and wealth creation strategies. He has been successful in some difficult tax-saving strategies and generally assisting clients with problem issues.

He holds a practising certificate with Chartered Accountants Australia New Zealand and an SMSF specialisation. In his 40 years of public practice, he has established and operated over 15 successful businesses, including a number of accounting practices, a finance company, a financial services company, and a sawmill.

Owning a business is not always a bed of roses – it takes dedicated effort, hard work and also *smart* work. But if you make it profitable, it is certainly very exciting. As a published author of numerous books and articles, Allan has been able to pass on that knowledge to help business owners achieve their aims.

When Allan was engaged by Kerry Packer at Consolidated Press Holdings, Kerry said, 'Son, you need to be worth double what I pay you.' That message has continued to resonate.

Allan can be contacted at www.allanmason.com.au.

## ALSO BY THE AUTHOR

*Survival to Success: How to Play the Game of Life and Win*

*Business Bullseye: How to Succeed in Business*

*How to Choose an Accountant: Your Most Valuable Team Member*

*Fable of a Master: Unleashing the Power that Lies within Us All*

*Tax Secrets of the Rich 2025–26*

For more information on these titles,
see www.broadviewpublishing.com.au

# PROPERTY $ECRET$ OF THE RICH

BY KERRY PACKER'S FORMER ACCOUNTANT ALLAN MASON

HarperCollins*Publishers*

**IMPORTANT NOTE**
The information in this book is intended as a general resource only and may not take account of your individual circumstances. You should consult a qualified professional before making financial decisions based on this book. To the maximum extent permitted by law, the author and publisher disclaim all responsibility and liability to any person, arising directly or indirectly from any person taking or not taking action based on the information in this publication.

**HarperCollins*Publishers***
Australia • Brazil • Canada • France • Germany • Holland • India
Italy • Japan • Mexico • New Zealand • Poland • Spain • Sweden
Switzerland • United Kingdom • United States of America

HarperCollins acknowledges the Traditional Custodians of the land upon which we live and work, and pays respect to Elders past and present.

First published on Gadigal Country in Australia in 2025
by HarperCollins*Publishers* Australia Pty Limited
ABN 36 009 913 517
harpercollins.com.au



HarperCollins Publishers
Macken House
39/40 Mayor Street Upper
Dublin 1, D01 C9W8, Ireland

A catalogue record for this book is available from the National Library of Australia

ISBN 978 1 4607 6819 8 (paperback)
ISBN 978 1 4607 1897 1 (ebook)

Cover design by Mietta Yans, HarperCollins Design Studio
Cover image by istockphoto.com
Author photograph by Brooke Mason Photography
Typeset in Sabon LT Std by Kirby Jones
Printed and bound in Australia by McPherson's Printing Group

## Dedication

We all want to retire young, make lots of money and pay less tax. My life experience and over 40 years in practice as a chartered accountant – which included working for the late Kerry Packer, who, at that time, was Australia's richest man – was so unique, I have an obligation to share Kerry's, plus the many other clients I have worked with, philosophy on tax and wealth creation.

As an accountant for over two decades, I have been privileged to gain an insight into the business world. I have seen over this period the effect of many decisions, some good and some bad. While I have been on the forefront of the taxation effect of many of those decisions, the lessons learned can be of value to us all, case studies of actual situations that the average person would never see, especially now with the benefit of hindsight.

I also wish to thank my wife, Marsha, for putting up with me for over 40 years. Yes, there were some highs and some lows, not to mention the long hours at the office.

Lastly, I want to thank my many clients, who have been far more than clients. In many cases, they have become lifelong friends. I have loved working with you and loved being challenged to find solutions.

# Contents

# Preface

Australians have a love affair with property. More than any other country, home ownership in Australia is one of the highest in the world. Even with the current boom in property and housing shortages (at the time of writing), this is still the case. Investors with large property portfolios are currently increasing their portfolios notwithstanding a push by the government to increase supply.

The reason is very simple. Property is a very tax-friendly investment. This is because of four distinct incentives:

1. Your sole and principal residence is tax free, so while you maintain that status, any gains you make will be tax free.
2. Gains made on the sale of investment property presently receive a 50 per cent CGT discount, meaning only half of any gain is taxed. As well as this, tax is only paid when the asset is sold. If you never sell, no tax is payable.
3. Due to what is often referred to as negative gearing, rental or other trading losses can be offset to other income or carried forward to future tax years, which lends itself to 'tax creativity'. This is often not the case with other types of losses that may be quarantined (under the non-

commercial loss rules in Division 35 of the *Income Tax Assessment Act 1997*), or treated as capital losses and only offset to capital gains.

4. And there are tricks associated with structuring and leverage that create massive financial and tax advantages.

In this book I will outline how you, the reader, can do exactly that. If you are employed, this may be your only road to wealth creation. In many cases, your only option might be how to use the incentives contained within the tax system to create wealth for your future.

While there has been some pressure to change the law regarding negative gearing, the government at this time has stated categorically that it will not change it. At the time of writing, I have assumed the government's promises on this will be maintained.

The government can at any time change the tax laws. This book has been written based on the law as it stands at the time of writing. Readers should always check the current laws in this area in case they have changed.

# Part 1

# Property as a vehicle to creating wealth

Property is not the only method to become wealthy, but it generally beats other methods. Every week, thousands of people buy lotto tickets with this same aim. They invest in many 'get rich quick' schemes, buy cryptocurrency, buy shares or many other assets. We have recently been receiving calls from people that have invested small sums (that they do not have) in schemes that promise returns of over 100 times their investment. The calls to our office are tax related and asking for assistance about how to manage the tax effect of the massive wealth they are about to receive. Sadly, these people will probably lose their entire investment and become extremely despondent for being so gullible.

Of course, some people do win lotto, some receive a return from an overseas philanthropic scheme and some manage to buy a cryptocurrency portfolio at an all-time low, trade it and make money.

As an accountant, I see the truth: the share trading that made massive capital losses, the investments that never came off. In my career, to be blunt, lotto or investment type schemes rarely succeed. I can say, unequivocally, the truth is that it is very rare for any of the above to actually yield a retirement income that will allow the investor to quit their day job or allow the pensioner to buy a house that they never thought possible. Their dreams are generally shattered.

The saying goes that if it sounds too good to be true, it generally is not true. Also, there is no short cut to wealth. It takes time and perseverance.

However, with solid assets like property, usually the tools are in your hands to create wealth. I will not say it will always work. There are traps for the uninitiated. There are errors you can make. Do not be naive. Do not blindly follow what a real estate agent or property developer advises. Be intelligent and make informed decisions. Take control, remove any rose-coloured glasses, use the tax system to give you a leg up and then use it to minimise any tax payable. Use the power of time and compounding to your advantage. According to surveys by HSBS, expats ranked Australia as the number 2 place to live and work in 2021. This is up from eighth position in 2020. In 2023, immigration to Australia was around 660,000. It will only get higher. No wonder the Australian property market continues to surge. The world has a love affair with Australia and this is expected to continue, which means house prices should stay high. But no one knows for certain: time and history will tell.

If we look at the past 30 years, owning a property portfolio has certainly been a very fruitful endeavour. This is how you can be assured that your road will lead you to being able to tell the government, when you reach pension age, 'No, thanks, I am good.'

1

# The importance of tax planning

**MYTH**

The more money I make, the more tax I pay.

To build a large property portfolio, you need to use the tax system and the tax breaks to help you. But before we cover how to do this, I felt it necessary to dispel some myths about taxation. The aim is to use it as a tool and not be a victim of the tax system. Of course, in reality, there will be times where you will be subject to paying tax that is unavoidable. With careful planning, you should be able to limit these times.

One big myth is 'the more money I make, the more tax I pay'. This is simply not true. Of course, those who expect businesses to pay their fair share, the tax office and other people who are suppressed by the system all believe this. But I can say that, as an accountant in both public practice and working in industry, there are often many ways around this. Call them loopholes of the rich and famous, if you like. I prefer to simply say: use the system to your advantage.

Let me first explain some simple examples of why the above is not true. Hint: consider the tax-planning aspects of these (which will be covered later in this book):

- In Australia, (in most cases) you do not pay tax on gains associated with your sole and principal residence.
- A small business (as defined) can elect to be taxed on a cash basis, which means invoices for work done that are not paid are not taxed until the money is received.
- You do not pay capital gains tax (CGT) on any increase in the value of motor vehicles.
- You only pay tax when a gain is realised; in other words, when you sell the asset.
- Capital gains on the sale of an investment property or other investment asset may be eligible for a 50 per cent CGT discount if you hold it for more than 12 months (hint, hint).
- Capital gains on the sale of a business may be eligible for a 50 per cent active asset discount.
- Capital gains on the sale of a business may be rolled over into superannuation to make the gain tax free (subject to certain rules). This can even eliminate the balance of any gain after the active asset discount.
- A superannuation fund pays no tax on income earned or capital gains when in pension mode. If in accumulation mode, the tax is limited to 15 per cent on income and 10 per cent on capital gains (again subject to various rules).

These are examples of some of the concessions available. It is a summary and does not cover all situations, as there are many more concessions available, where profits are not taxed. Every situation is different, and concessions can be lost if you are not careful. For instance, if your sole and principal residence is rented out or you move overseas, the above concession can be reduced or lost entirely.

The main point is that just because you earn income, it is not true that you will always be taxed on it.

That is why I stress that you need to be on the front foot with tax planning. Clever structuring and planning can reduce and, in some cases, eliminate any tax payable. For example, capital gains are only taxable if you sell. Hence, you would be crazy to sell an asset if you knew that in a particular tax year your income will be high. Wouldn't it make sense to limit your other income (say, from your business) if you were faced with a capital gain in a particular year? Also in the year of any capital gain, you may consider making extra superannuation payments, even bringing forward any prior year underpayments (subject to the caps). You may also consider prepaying a full year's interest on another investment property. As stated, these are only a few of the concessions available. There are many more.

To repeat something Kerry Packer said before a Senate inquiry, 'the government doesn't spend my money too wisely, therefore I am not paying a cent more tax than absolutely necessary.' It is not how much money you make that is important; it is how much you keep. With the top tax rate as high as 47 per cent, it can become hard to get ahead. It can be hard to manage your affairs so that you keep below the tax thresholds or to save for your future retirement.

Having had Kerry Packer and many other high-net-worth people as clients, I know what these people think about tax, and how they use the system to their advantage. They never accept the status quo or that nothing can be done; they always look for an advantage, and challenge their advisors to find a way around to make the system work for them.

We all know that not one system fits all. To be effective, you need to know how to use the tax system. Let me give you some simple examples on how you can tailor a transaction in accordance with the system.

First, some simple rules. In most cases, you pay tax on realised gains, not unrealised, so you have a chance to defer the taxing point.

Second, all expenses incurred in earning that assessable income are generally deductible.

Third, there are many tax exemptions that can apply, including prepayment rules, CGT discounts, repairs needed to restore a rental property to its former condition, sole and principal residence exemptions, and so on.

Fourth, a superannuation fund is a tax-effective environment. Hence, it may make sense to keep any high-profit assets in your super fund. For example, we had a client that was given shares in a company (shortly to be listed) that he had an association with. The exercise price was way below the expected listing price. It made sense to put these shares into his super fund. Also be aware that you can catch up on any shortfall in concessional superannuation contributions up to the annual caps for five years. There are rules on this, of course, but it may help offset any unexpected gains on other assets that may occur in a particular year.

Fifth, be aware of the various rollover provisions if you sell a business and the provisions associated with scrip for scrip rollovers. They defer or even eliminate any capital gain. Rollover provisions can also be used if you inherit a property and hold it, rather than sell. If you rollover a capital gain into superannuation and you do not pay tax on that gain, it may be useful to use that money to buy property in your super fund. This is a good way to build up your superannuation balances in a tax-free environment (subject, of course, to various limits).

My point is that you need to stand back from a transaction. For example, why do repairs on your rental property in a year when your income is low? Do them when the tax benefit is greatest. Think about better ways to handle what you intend on doing and the concessions that may be available to reduce any taxes payable. Amend the structure of the transaction if you can. Be proactive and get advice early. Don't hand to your accountants a fait accompli. Involve them in the early stages. Quite simply, that is how the wealthy reduce their tax. They plan, get advice and amend as needed.

## 2

# How to create wealth – the strategy

As an accountant in public practice, I would be doing my clients and readers a disservice if I did not pass on my many years of wisdom and the trial-and-error lessons learned from a life in the financial (and tax) world.

If you wish to create wealth by building an asset portfolio, the only way is through gearing and using the increases that occur in both the property market and share markets over time. I will discuss how the tax office can help you do this later.

Before I get to the meat in the sandwich, I want to recap why it is important to plan ahead and how this philosophical strategy works. Later in this book, I will get into the detail. This philosophical strategy is actually what most people do, who have created wealth, even though they don't realise it. Yes, there are those that have created a massive business. Or won lotto. But the average wealthy person has followed the strategy detailed here, even those who are employed and do not have the advantages of those who are in business and are therefore able to use the tax system the way a business owner can. Those in employment can use negative gearing to help achieve their goals.

Let me talk about the landscape we all live in. You work or run a business or are employed on a large salary. The ATO takes about one-third to one-half, so the balance is what you have left to deal with. To build wealth, you need to follow a savings pattern to give you a deposit or somehow take a leap of faith and borrow to the hilt. In other words, you use other people's money, gearing and prepayments to give you a tax refund boost and all the things mentioned in this book.

For example, in 1991, I was facing a huge tax bill. The year hadn't ended so I had time. I fixed this problem by purchasing a small block of units at Campsie and paying one year's interest in advance prior to 30 June. This action completely eliminated any tax liability.

For your first purchase you need to save somewhere around 20 per cent of the purchase price. This is the hard part, the part where most people simply never get. If it was easy, everyone would do it. This is where you separate yourself from the pack. In the chapter on compounding and the chapters that follow, you will see how this gets easier. In Robert Kiyosaki's book *Rich Dad Poor Dad*, he covers why this first step is so important. It will be how you break the poverty trap.

Now comes the tricky part. The part that no one tells you about. That is luck and timing. People tell you how smart they are with investing, but in most cases there is an element of luck. In truth, you cannot predict the economy. You cannot predict a recession, pandemic or financial crisis. You need to be careful. If you take the above path and the economy throws you a curveball, stand up and dust yourself off and try again. It happens. It doesn't always happen and is perhaps a once in a five- or ten-year event. Step back and do it again. Don't be disillusioned and throw the towel into the ring. Don't complain that you can never be wealthy. Do not give up. Treat it as an education exercise.

So now I have dealt with the negative, the reality of life and why some people trip over and never pick themselves up. However, those that are lucky enough to not trip, that are able to time the first couple of foundation building steps, never look back. Also be aware that time will often fix those poor timing issue. Be patient: don't lose your nerve and sell at a loss.

Let me now cover the true message of this chapter with a simple example that will explain what most people have done to create wealth. Believe me, it is not rocket science.

I will use some simple numbers that make it easy to follow. Let us assume that you wish to create a $10 million portfolio. It doesn't matter whether it is shares or property, but you want to create an asset portfolio. Assets that history shows will increase and be stable and income earning, and that the income earned will cover any holding costs. Let's use property, as that is easy to visualise, but I have seen people do it with share portfolios. Every year they buy more and more blue chip shares, such as Commonwealth Bank and BHP. There is an example in the chapter about share investing, where Mrs G did this for 30 years and now has a portfolio that is worth in excess of $7 million, with a cost base of $2 million, and earns $300,000 per annum in dividends, mostly franked.

The strategy is simple with these steps:

1. It doesn't matter how much borrowing you have as long as the income covers the interest and repayments, or you can structure the asset that way. Remember, the bigger

the base, the larger the gains will be due to asset growth, inflation and so on. It will also magnify the losses if you get it wrong.

2. Assume that in some years, using the gross asset base of $10 million, it grows 3 per cent – that's a gain of $300,000 for doing nothing.
3. In some years, you will get a 5–8 per cent increase, making $500,000 to $800,000. In a ten-year period, there will often be great years where the returns will be 20 per cent. There may be a road bump where the values drop. But if you look at any chart, even over the past 100 years, the trend will always be up. For example, the average house price in Sydney in 1970 was $18,700. It is now in excess of $1.5 million. Commonwealth Bank shares when it listed in 1991 were $9.00, and they are now over $140.00.
4. Compounding the above in five years, your asset base should grow by about 50 per cent, or $5,000,000. If you have debt, you may wish to sell down some assets to reduce it, but maybe not. When you sell to pay down debt, you crystallise a capital gain and there will be tax consequences. The smart thing to do is to use the increased equity to increase your asset base. The important part is having a large enough asset pool or base that a small increase will give you massive returns. Hence, 5 per cent on $10 million will give you a $500,000 gain, or another way to look at it is a $500,000 income. An unrealised and therefore tax-free gain.
5. Be clever about selling down as tax will be payable. Use the CGT concessions and the prepayment rules (for

interest in advance on other properties) to their max. But hopefully you will have amassed enough wealth that you do not care.

6. I guarantee you, barring a recession, if you hold this course your $10 million geared property or share portfolio will turn into a $10 million net worth. You will never need to work again, and reap the benefits. In Part 3, I have prepared a number of futuristic projections on what this could look like and how to amass a $24 million portfolio, from a $200,000 initial investment.

How do you create the above $10 million portfolio? Firstly, you do it a year or two at a time. Every couple of years you buy an asset, which will be geared maybe to 80 per cent. Use the tax system to help you. How do you fund that first purchase? As mentioned earlier, this is the hardest step. It will be what differentiates you, the future wealth builder, from the average person that talks but never acts, the person who others will envy and say you are just lucky. You will need to scrimp and save, get help, and find a way, but do it. Borrow on your house, do what it takes. Then over the next five years you continue purchasing and don't sell. You may hit some roadblocks or poor timing issues, but in time these will smooth themselves out. Look back and you can see that with every bump in the road, there were smooth waters ahead. Hold your cool.

I know you are thinking, 'This looks easy, so why doesn't everybody do it?' I can tell you a lot of people do exactly this. They don't brag and tell others, except their accountants (me) so I see it. They have that quiet financially independent smile on their face. Life is now easy for them. I know because I have also done it.

A word of warning: don't let yourself be talked into buying overpriced assets. Take off any rose-coloured glasses. Watch out for financial advisors that are trying to sell you overpriced property that earns them a massive commission. Don't buy shares at the top of the market when the index is overheated. Don't rush, but don't sit on the fence either. Do your homework and be intelligent about what you buy. But also act. Timing and holding on to assets for a long period will always yield rewards. It was Kenneth Fisher who said, 'It is time in the market rather than timing the market that matters.'

Why doesn't everybody follow this strategy? Some are simply afraid to step outside their comfort zone. They follow the masses, who do not think intelligently. They talk to the wrong people, have the wrong financial mentors, do not read self-help books, do not invest in their own financial education and then complain they are poor. Then they justify their poor life strategy by telling others that we are all meant to live in poverty. They follow those that hit a road bump on the way and have let themselves sink into depression and a 'poor me' type financial attitude. They have become suppressed by the system and never recovered. If this is you, isn't it time to change? To rethink your assumptions about life and wealth?

In this world there are two kinds of people: those that let money control them and those that control money. The moment you let money control you, you become a slave to the system. Creating wealth is not about having more money, but having *control* over your money, your time and your life. To do this, you must create a passive cash flow income: income that is generating without using your limited time.

Businessman and philanthropist Warren Buffett said, 'If you don't find a way to make money while you sleep, you will work until you die.' Building a large property or share portfolio will eventually give you that passive income you need to quit your day job.

If you want to create your own life of abundance, do what the wealthy do (and not the poor). These are the self-funded retirees that you never hear about. They quietly get on with life, drive their nice cars, have nice motor homes and travel the country.

In 2024, Finder commissioned a survey of 1008 Australians who are actively increasing their wealth through investments in various assets. Astonishingly, one in eight Australians – roughly 2.8 million people – are millionaires, one of the highest proportions globally. Many of these millionaires have landed in this once-elusive club simply because the value of their homes has grown. The number of millionaires drops to 1.1 million when the value of the principal place of residence is removed from net wealth calculations. Aussie investors with more than $1 million in net wealth are much more likely to have at least one passive income source. While money or the lack of it, can be a source of stress, most people are curious as to how others have been able to become financially secure. Of course, you should never live beyond your means nor stretch yourself (financially) so far that you risk losing everything. But adopting some of the habits of the wealthy can help. These are habits relating to spending and how you invest. By following these habits, it can help you achieve the same financial freedom no matter how much you earn. After all, in many cases these wealthy people were, at one time, just like you – searching for answers, trying to become financially secure. Building wealth and achieving financial security is still a top priority of many Australians.

*

In their book *The Millionaire Next Door*, Thomas J Stanley and William D Danko talk about these real millionaires who quietly get on with their lives, are debt free, stress free and in charge of their own time. They do whatever they wish because they have the freedom to do so. They quietly tell the government what they can do with their meagre pension and go about living a life in the manner that we all aspire to. Simple, but a reality.

3

# Ten tips on how to break the poverty trap

In the previous chapter, I covered the strategy to follow to live a life of abundance. However, it is a fact that many people live from one pay period to the next, especially early in their working life. Even worse, there has been a massive increase in pay cheque lending. Some people, sadly, need to borrow against their next week's (or month's) income. In Australia, it is estimated that 48.4 per cent of the population live pay week to pay week. Australia is not alone in this. In the United States of America, a crazy 64.4 per cent of Americans fit into this category. While that's challenging enough, many also have trouble paying their bills. Also alarmingly, some 16.2 per cent have less than $1000 in savings (or 3.4 million people). Imagine what would happen if they lost their job. This could cause homelessness.

While many factors contribute to financial struggles, there are numerous reasons that keep you from building wealth. In his book, Robert Kiyosaki identified some of these. Warren Buffett and Earl Nightingale also outlined these reasons, which I will summarise below.

Since you are reading this book, you will not be one of them because you are taking the time and effort to educate yourself. I congratulate you. But there are still things to learn. The greatest barrier to knowledge is thinking you know it all, so be open to new ideas.

## 1 Not making saving a priority

Most people approach saving the wrong way. They save what they have left rather than setting savings as a priority. Money is like water on the pavement. If you leave it there, it will evaporate. If you leave it in your account, you will find something to spend it on. The solution lies in automating your savings immediately after receiving your income. Treat savings as a non-negotiable expense, an amount set aside that is transferred immediately on receipt (like tax). You will soon get used to the lower amount. This will create a foundation for wealth building and ensure consistent progress towards your financial goals. Any other approach typically results in minimal or zero savings, and so you never break free of the poverty cycle.

## 2 Unnecessary spending habits

This is the McMansion scenario. You get a pay rise and immediately go out and buy a new house or new car. It is so easy to fall victim to lifestyle inflation, increasing your spending as your income rises. It creates a cycle of consumption that prevents wealth accumulation. Again, Robert Kiyosaki talks about this when he says his poor dad (a university professor) earns a high income but never has any money left over. When he gets a raise, he increases his mortgage by buying a new car or new house. Tax, of course, is a never-ending story of cutting into any salary increase to keep you in poverty (due to bracket creep).

You must distinguish between what you really need or you simply want to own. Make conscious purchase decisions in alignment with your goals. Eliminate unnecessary spending on consumable items, eliminate what Robert Kiyosaki calls bad debt (credit card spending, Afterpay, etc). This will free up spending to enable saving for investment. It will also help create an emergency savings nest egg in case you become unemployed or incapacitated. It will also help you break free of the 'working for a living' trap.

## 3 Delayed investment decisions (procrastination)

Compounding, which is using time, is a vital part of wealth creation. Even if you buy at the wrong time in a property cycle, eventually time will fix the problem. Yet many people postpone investing until they feel 'ready'. This delay costs them years of potential compound growth. I mention compounding many times, as it is so important in creating wealth. People delay their decision for all sorts of reasons, many of which seem valid, like starting a family or waiting for the right property, a bargain or a property downturn. But in truth, this procrastination can cost you dearly in the compounding cycle and actually be an extremely expensive action.

Even with small amounts, starting early allows your money to work harder for you. For example, a 25-year-old investing $200 per month could accumulate significantly more by retirement than someone who starts at 35, even if the latter invests more each month. Assuming a compounding rate of 7 per cent, the person who started at 25 will have 40 years to retirement and have accumulated $525,082. The 35-year-old, if they double the investment to $400.00 per month, still won't catch up and will only have $486,538, even though they contributed an extra $48,000.

The 35-year-old delayed their investment by ten years, tried to catch up but couldn't. They invested an extra $48,000 but still ended up $38,544 behind.

## 4 Underinvestment in self-development

While financial education in schools and university is sadly lacking, there are numerous self-help books out there. After all, what better way to spend your time than investing in yourself, and in how to have a self-fulfilling life free from the burden of working for someone else. Free from selling your limited time for a small reward and free from the shackles of reporting to someone else. If that doesn't get your attention, think about your family. Imagine being able to afford an education for your children so that they can attend a school of their choice.

While you may wish to simply focus on investing (taking a short cut), you must never neglect your own financial literacy. If it was easy, everyone would do it. There are many people are out there that will give you advice that may not be in your best interests, or worse, are in the advisor's (income) interest. Additional education, new skills and professional development can help you make your own choices and decisions. It will also increase your earning potential. This might mean taking courses, obtaining certifications or learning new technologies. Many of the strategies outlined in this book will often require you to increase your income. This may mean getting a better job or creating a business on the side. Education can be the tool to help achieve these aims. The return on investment for self-development will always exceed traditional investment returns, as enhanced skills can lead to higher income throughout your career, which may span as much as 50 years.

## 5 Poor or limited financial education

You increase your risk exponentially when you enter into a decision without full knowledge of what you are doing. Financial illiteracy leads to poor decision making and missed opportunities. Understanding basic concepts like compound interest, diversification and risk management are crucial for building wealth.

Many people make financial decisions without adequate knowledge, leading to costly mistakes. Learning financial basics can significantly improve your ability to grow and preserve your wealth. Also be careful about the so-called experts that advise you on what to do. For example, would you take advice from a financial planner that doesn't even own their home or that has no life experience? Would you take advice from those claiming to be experts on Facebook or TikTok? The latter promoted a scheme on how to get a GST refund on the basis that the government wanted to help small business owners. The scheme said that small business owners could register for an ABN and GST, claim a GST refund of up to $100,000 of input credits, and that the government would happily give you the refund. Those that followed this advice are now facing criminal prosecution and, if the government did release the money, are being sued to repay it. If they can't repay the false claim, they will have a tax debt, accruing interest for a long time into the future.

## 6 Bad spending habits

Poor spending habits are costly. It may be that daily coffee, smoking, drinking at the club, poker machine addiction, that Saturday flutter on the horses or buying lottery tickets. These habits compound over time, forming habits that can build or destroy wealth. The compounding effect over a lifetime can even be the reason that you cannot save that initial deposit on your first home or investment property. Make a deliberate decision to break free and replace poor habits with habits that will form the foundation of your future wealth-building success. This is what will distinguish you from the masses, as you will create sufficient passive income to never need to work again.

## 7 'Get rich quick' mentality

Be careful about those spruiking quick success or gains. Risk increases with return. Instead, settle on more stable and low-risk investments. Overnight wealth often leads to risky investments and poor financial decisions. Never gamble on speculative investments or fall for schemes promising quick returns. This is covered later. But remember, the chances of winning lotto is in excess of 1 in 30 million. The same applies to most 'get rich quick' schemes.

Wealth building requires a consistent approach using proven strategies such as regular investing, diversification and patience, rather than seeking dramatic short-term gains.

## 8 Not fully appreciating or using the power of compounding gains

Many people underappreciate the power of compound interest. When income generates its own returns, wealth can grow exponentially over time. A $10,000 investment earning 8 per cent annually becomes $46,610 after 20 years through compound interest. Most people never grasp the power of compounding capital because they just can't see it. They focus on short-term gains rather than the big picture. Understanding compound interest at an early age can really ensure you will have enough income to retire on when in your 50s or 60s. This is why you need to use the power of compounding. This is covered in more detail in a later chapter, as it is so important to grasp.

## 9 Not managing your debt

The world, including Australia, is experiencing high interest rates. For many, this increase will create a massive drain on your wealth and a burden on your household budget. Before you embark on any wealth creation strategy, ensure you consider the negative side of what can go wrong. For example, banks always factor in rate increases and test your repayment sensitively to rate increases. You must be able to afford your investments and ensure you take a balanced approached to wealth creation, an approach that, over time, will be strategic and balanced.

A problem of Western society is credit card debt. Advertising and pressure to keep up with your friends and neighbours will test your financial resolve. Many will stay poor because they cannot pass up the opportunity to buy the next best consumable item. They continue the cycle by making the minimum payments. The result is a cycle of financial struggle, one that offers little room to break free, like a mouse on a wheel. There is no capacity left to save for that first investment property. They are now prohibited from creating their path to financial freedom, all because of bad financial habits and bad debt management. I know that may sound harsh, but unfortunately it is a sad reality for most people. Breaking free requires breaking those bad habits.

## 10 Lack of financial planning

I have many clients who are high-income earners, like doctors or lawyers. They often struggle to build wealth because they do not have clear financial goals. They never sit back and think about a future plan. Decisions are made based on 'must haves', what everyone else has and instant gratification. They buy expensive cars, nice homes to live in, have high mortgages (on their home) and have big taxation with very few write-offs.

A financial plan may mean that you need to give up certain short-term purchases. It will provide direction to help you make decisions that align with your long-term goals. It may include not living on the best street, but saving for investment properties, or not owning the latest car. It will include setting targets for savings, investing, debt reduction and retirement.

By regularly reviewing and adjusting your plan, you will ensure you stay on track towards financial success. Plan on paper before you embark on any strategy. Put away a regular savings amount before you spend it. It is the only way to create a nest egg that will guarantee financial freedom. Remember the Robert Kiyosaki example in *Rich Dad Poor Dad*. Robert's role model lived in an old, poorly maintained house until he built his investment portfolio to a level that he could afford to buy the best house on the street with no debt.

## Conclusion

Creating financial freedom is not about making extraordinary moves or having special privileges. You need to follow sound financial principles and be constant over time. Avoid the mistakes listed here that will keep you in poverty.

Implement financial wisdom. Think of your life like a business that you want to grow and become self-sustaining, like an ASX-listed company that will pay you a dividend every year without having to use your time to achieve it. This will allow you to break free from any limitations that working for a living creates.

Start by breaking any bad habits that are not aligned with these goals. Be patient and disciplined. Avoid the mistakes so many people make that will keep them shackled to a life of poverty.

4

# Why property is the favoured option

The big question in building wealth for the future is, 'Why buy property?' Financial planners will (with some degree of truth) tell you that residential property will yield only about 3.5 per cent, commercial property about 6.5 per cent and dividends from shares can be as high as 9 per cent, so the maths is generally skewed to share portfolios.

The truth is that most small-time investors will make their money from residential property. I know I have. Businesses and other investments just help fuel the main game.

The points that this pure mathematical equation above miss is that of the following:

1. You can leverage property investing such that the investment may be only 20 per cent of the purchase price (or less). If the property doubles from, say, $500,000 to $1,000,000, your investment of $100,000 has yielded a gain of $500,000, five times the investment. Yes, I know the same holds true for commercial property and shares. But banks are loath to lend on these assets.

2. You can use leverage to assist with massive tax deductions in the early years of acquisition and hence the ATO can help you fund the costs associated with this investment. This is especially true if you are employed and paying high taxes.
3. Property will also yield a strong return. The right property will stand the test of time and always be in demand.
4. Property can be improved, subdivided or changed to increase its value.

A point I often make to clients is that in life you need to have three horses in the journey to financial freedom. The first is your home, which will increase in value and be a great part of wealth creation, not to mention a tax-free investment.

The second is what you do for a living, your job, which will provide the fuel to keep the horse moving and create opportunities. This horse needs to be fed, needs to look like a thoroughbred and be capable of giving you that initial start. It will be what banks look at when they provide the loans you need to start this journey. It will be your fallback safety net if things go wrong, like spikes in interest rates or other road bumps you encounter.

The third is your investments, which will create the long-term wealth to enable you to stable the second horse when it no longer has the energy to run fast. When the second horse is ready to be put out to pasture, the third horse will become the main winner in the future that will stand out from your first and second horse and help you win the race to financial freedom.

We all have the third horse (or plank) of wealth creation via our superannuation. But you need to do more. Superannuation at

11.5 per cent (increasing to 12 per cent on 1 July 2025) of your salary, less all the fees and charges the fund will take, is simply not enough to create any sizeable nest egg to give you the retirement benefit you need to live a life of abundance. You need to take wealth creation seriously. With house prices averaging 5.4 per cent gains every year for the past 50 years, and with Sydney house prices rising from $18,700 to over $1.5 million in the same period, it is hard to go past property as a vehicle for long-term growth.

Your challenge will be how to change your spending habits and savings pattern to start this journey to build a property portfolio; how to focus on what is important to you and not allow yourself to be sidetracked in making the wrong spending decisions. And how to use compounding to create the life of abundance we all seek to achieve.

## 5

# Where should I buy and why?

When embarking on a wealth-building strategy for the future, you need to remain cautious about any 'get rich quick' schemes. This applies equally to property as with any other investments. There is an old rule that the longer an asset exists, the more likely it is to continue. Warren Buffett, for example, only buys shares in companies that have stood the test of time and have been around for a long period, often household names like Coca-Cola. This is called the Lindy effect. The Lindy effect proposes the longer a period something has survived/existed or is used in the present, the longer its remaining life expectancy will be. In other words, assets that are low risk. Remember the dot-com boom. Many of those companies do not exist today.

Real estate agents always talk about the three keys to choosing the right property. Their motto is location, location, location. In terms of the Lindy effect, that means property that is in well-established areas. Not in mining towns that may be experiencing a temporary boom, but close to capital cities where they have infrastructure and are always in demand. Somewhere within, say, a 15-kilometre radius of a major town or capital city. The adage that land is the one asset that they are not making any more of applies here, especially close to capital cities. It doesn't apply to regional areas that only need a rezoning of farmland to increase supply. The other criteria to look for is up-and-coming areas, meaning areas that are likely to improve, often referred to as gentrification. Examples are Newtown or Redfern in Sydney, or New Farm in Brisbane. Again, in areas close to a capital city with good infrastructure, like transport hubs, schools and hospitals.

In building my portfolio, I purchased two properties at Redbank Plains. These were two standalone houses in a strata complex. They were brand new and so I had depreciation claims. They were really great little two- and three-bedroom houses with yards plus all conveniences in the complex, such as a pool. But Redbank Plains is not exactly Brisbane CBD. I found the quality of tenants was poor. Repairs, even though the properties were new, seemed to be ongoing. The cost of a dishwasher on a $400,000 home is relatively the same as the cost in a $1 million home. Redbank Plains is an up-and-coming new suburb. There is a lot of rural land that is slowly being rezoned. Hence supply tends to increase. After two years, I'd had enough. Tenants leaving or not paying their rent and repairs all made it high maintenance, so I sold them both.

My point is you cannot go wrong with good areas, even if you pay more. My other properties rarely ever give me any problems. Hence, my resolve to stick to better socioeconomic areas.

The other point I am often asked is whether your first property should be your home. This is covered in more detail in the next chapter. While your principal place of residence (PPR) might make sense from a personal point of view, it doesn't from a tax and investments point of view. All of the advantages of your PPR are that it is tax free when you sell it. But remember, we are trying to build a property portfolio for future income purposes and trying to get some subsidies from the taxation office via negative gearing. My view is that your first property should be your investment property. For example, in *Rich Dad Poor Dad*, Robert Kiyosaki states that his rich dad lived in the worst house on the street, a run-down house in a poor suburb, until he amassed a portfolio of properties to allow him to buy his first home with the minimum loan possible. I know that to the average person in 2025, this is probably not a palatable way to go. But I suggest, if young enough, you live with your parents until you can build enough equity to buy your forever home with very little or no non-deductible interest costs. But I also realise that many will not follow that path for personal reasons.

In respect to your forever home or your PPR, if and when you make that purchase, buy for all of the same reasons you would use for a rental property. These are close to schools, close to public transport and close to where you work. A daily commute that is tedious, time consuming and costly is never a good option.

In summary, when deciding where to buy property, you need to consider:

1. Do you buy an investment property or your forever home first?
2. If you must buy your forever home first, what other considerations are there to take into account, such as proximity to work, schools and transport?
3. If first buying an investment property, again, what areas do you pick that will give you the greatest gains?
4. What area do you choose for your forever home and when is the right time to buy?

6

# My first property – a home or an investment property?

As mentioned in the previous chapter, this is a common question and certainly not an easy one to answer. There are two competing aims:

1. To have a stable place to live that is not subject to landlord whims and a place to call home that will increase in value, with all increases in value being tax free.
2. The tax deductibility of the interest costs on the loan needed. In other words, the need to have the ATO subsidy to help you meet your repayments and to ultimately help you grow your asset base.

So which one is the clear winner? Let's examine the issues:

1. Are there personal lifestyle issues that take precedence? Is your home the most important thing in your life, at this time in your life? Can you wait?
2. What is your long-term aim? Is it a conservative life, with just a few properties? Do you fear debt such that you cannot sleep at night?

3. Are you trying to create wealth, prepared to take a risk and willing to do what it takes, even if in the short term it creates some pain? Even if, in the short term, your family life may suffer? Is your family supportive of your aims and goals?
4. What is your level of income and tax you pay? Are you earning a high wage? Are you determined to reduce the tax you pay?
5. Do you feel the starting point is at a difficult time and you want to be a little conservative?

Another factor is that rent as a return on capital is usually equivalent to about a 3.5 per cent return on your money, sometimes worse when there are repairs needed, so investment wise, rental income is a lot less than many other forms of investment. Without the tax advantages, the capital gains that result, you would actually be better investing your money with the bank at 5 per cent, on share index funds at about 9 per cent or in blue chip shares at around 8 per cent fully franked with franking credits. But we all know that long-term property is a more stable and better investment. Plus, it is easier to get right.

When we consider from a pure financial point of view whether you rent your first home or buy an investment property, owning investment properties will usually be the best course of action in the long term. In other words, in the short term you become both a tenant and a landlord.

Let me challenge some myths in this area. In Part 2 of this book, I cover the different strategies for a person in either their early working age, prime working age or mature working age (in their twilight years). They are different for everyone at different stages in their life. Those in the first two categories should have lots of debt and use the banks to assist with purchasing lots of properties. Those in their twilight years need to start transitioning into other forms of investment to reduce debt and be in retirement mode with more of their assets in superannuation, which is a low-tax environment.

Irrespective of your age group, the old adage that houses are for nesting, not investing, no longer applies. This implied that your first priority in life was your family home, and that you should pay off your mortgage before you considered purchasing other properties. To achieve this, you would typically take about 20 years to pay off your loan. This strategy was that then you could use that equity to buy your first investment property. Your parents probably said that to you. They probably followed that path. I am sure that now that you look at this from a purely financial point of view, you can see that it is flawed. Think of all the increases in property values that you will have missed out on in those 20 years of mortgage payments.

My parents were a prime example. They worked hard all their lives, bought a home, paid it off when they were in their 50s and then sold it to downsize and release the capital to help fund their retirement and lifestyle. Selling your family home once you've finally paid off the mortgage isn't success or freedom, nor is the dream of being mortgage free.

I mention a number of times in this book the concept of good and bad debt. This was something Robert Kiyosaki discussed. The old way of thinking was that all debt is bad. The first thing you must do is pay it off because the banks are evil and not to be trusted, and you do not want to be at their mercy. But the reverse is actually true. Alan Bond, an entrepreneur of the 1980s, often said that if you owed the bank enough, then they could never foreclose on you. Then, of course, the ATO added their views. The new norm that the banks and the ATO want you to work under is to pay the ATO, pay your mortgage and then live with whatever is left over.

Frankly, this is a recipe for retiring broke, a recipe for being dependent upon the government for a meagre pension and living in a retirement home in your twilight years, with no debt, but no assets either. A recipe of suppression and control.

This is an old belief system that does not apply in today's fast moving world, when the deposit gap grows so fast that you are always chasing it. To obtain financial freedom, you need to make your money work harder. Use the system, like tax incentives, depreciation, gearing and the power of time. Investing for the future by buying more properties (or even other asset classes) is far better than servicing one mortgage, namely your home loan.

The other factor is that debt becomes less relevant over time due to inflation. For example, in 1971 if you borrowed $18,700 for your first home in Sydney and still owed $18,700 in 2025, would that matter on a $1.5 million home? The same would apply if you borrowed $1 million in 2025, and in 2055 you still owed $1 million on a property that, based on 5 per cent growth, was now worth nearly $4 million. The strategy instead is to use the equity in your mortgages to buy more investment properties because, quite simply, the more properties you own, the greater your exposure to long-term property growth.

You just need to change your thinking about debt and use it as a method to accelerate your wealth. Always be careful that you do not slip up and become a victim of the banks. Always ensure one way or another you can meet your commitments. Review Chapter 16 on some of the mistakes I have seen clients make. In Part 2 of this book, I outline a strategy that is staged over a period of time. Not a 'get rich quick' system. After all, I am an accountant and I am supposed to be conservative.

Going back to the original question, should your first home be a rental property or your forever home? Financially, it should be an investment property. In fact, as mentioned in the earlier chapter, if you are in the early working age category and you can live with your parents and also buy your first investment property, that is even better. Imagine, instead of paying off your home over 20 years, you used that money to buy four more properties. The projections in Part 2 show clearly the effect of that strategy. It is a $9.2 million effect. Imagine what you could do with that extra money. Imagine the new home you could buy debt free with that return.

# Part 2

# Strategies for different stages of life

What strategy would I tell my 20-, 30-, 40- or 50-year-old self, with the benefit of hindsight? What should someone struggling to make ends meet do? What does a person on a high salary, paying exorbitant tax do? What would someone moving closer to retirement do? These are all good questions that need answering. The answer and strategies are different for every age segment. However, some basic truths remain the same.

You may be in any of the above phases of your life. You may be thinking it is too late to enter the property market. I hear this every day: 'I wish I had told my young self to buy such and such', 'I wish I never sold that property in Earlwood that I paid $26,000 for in the late 1980s'. Isn't hindsight a wonderful thing?

But let me say, it is never too late to begin this journey. When everyone says it is too late, when everyone says property is overpriced, it never is. I recall everyone saying the same thing back in the 1990s. Look at prices now. In your lifetime, you will encounter two to three massive property surges, then it will level off for a period. That is what happened in the past, and history always has a way of repeating itself. If you take a 30-year average, the mean property prices in Australia have grown at an annual growth rate of 5.4 per cent. The national median dwelling value has increased 382 per cent in this time. Nearly four times. In some places, this growth has been in excess of 1000 per cent.

In the following chapters, I have listed the assumptions and forecasts associated with those assumptions. I have then addressed what a person in the following three age categories should do:

- **Early working age:** 20–30 years of age
- **Prime working age:** 30–40 years of age
- **Mature working age:** 40–50 years of age

At various stages in life your priorities, objectives and aspirations will vary greatly. With the use of financial modelling, I have considered what the long-term effect of various financial decisions could be. Of course, the earlier you embark on a property journey, the better. But sometimes that is simply not possible. As you move into the later age categories (a polite way of saying 'as you get older') your focus will change.

In Chapter 7, I have outlined this modelling, the assumptions and the likely future effect. I have drawn on the past to try and predict what the future property market could look like in 20, 30 or 40 years, based on the past. Within those parameters, I have considered what someone in those aforementioned three categories of life should follow.

The results are astounding.

# 7

# Can I predict the future?

The past is usually a good indication of the future. There will always be curveballs and extraordinary events like the Covid-19 pandemic or war that change things, but generally in most cases you can use the past as a guide to the future.

Will property continue to rise as it has over the past three years or will it tank to the level that everyone will lose everything? No one knows for certain. But a look at the past 30 years (or even 100 years) shows that property has grown 5.4 per cent annually. Anecdotally, we all know that to be the case and can look back on past property sales and say, 'If only I still owned or purchased that property back then.'

As an accountant in public practice, investment questions come up continually. Should I sell, hold or buy more? Generally, my advice is to try and hold on as long as possible. You just never know when the next boom will be. If you need to sell, do not remain out of the market for any length of time, as sometimes change is hard to predict and getting back in may be more difficult. Change seems to creep up and before you know it you can be priced out of the market.

Over the next 20 years, no one can predict what the market will do with any certainty. Everywhere you look the figures vary.

In truth, no one actually knows what will happen. Eliza Owen, head of research at CoreLogic Australia in January 2025, prepared the following historical data in relation to the property market for 2020–2023. Head of Research at the ANZ Bank economist Madeline Dunk added these forecasts for 2024, 2025 and 2026.

**Figure 1 Historical data and forecasts for the Australian property market (%)**

| Year | Australia | Sydney | Melbourne | Brisbane | Adelaide | Perth | Hobart | Canberra | Darwin |
|---|---|---|---|---|---|---|---|---|---|
| 2020 | 3.40 | 2.70 | 0.80 | 4.70 | 5.40 | 9.30 | 7.80 | 9.40 | 8.30 |
| 2021 | 23.10 | 26.90 | 16.10 | 31.50 | 22.30 | 13.90 | 32.60 | 25.60 | 13.60 |
| 2022 | -6.40 | -11.40 | -7.10 | -1.90 | 9.30 | 4.20 | -6.80 | -3.10 | 2.30 |
| 2023 | 9.70 | 11.30 | 4.20 | 13.50 | 8.80 | 16.20 | -1.80 | 0.40 | 0.00 |
| 2024 (forecast) | 5.00 | 2.70 | -2.40 | 11.80 | 13.50 | 20.20 | -0.20 | 0.00 | -0.50 |
| 2025 (forecast) | 2.70 | 0.70 | 0.10 | 5.80 | 3.50 | 8.50 | 0.10 | -0.90 | 0.10 |
| 2026 (forecast) | 4.10 | 3.70 | 4.90 | 4.80 | 2.40 | 4.50 | 1.80 | 1.50 | 2.20 |

Source: CoreLogic (historical), ANZ Research (forecasts)

My personal take on the property market is that growth is never linear. In Figure 1, the increases Australia-wide varied from –6.4 per cent to +23.1 per cent. Remember that we are dealing with averages and statistics. The figures released each quarter are based on average sale prices in each capital city. Say, for example, in a period in question a massive number of high-end sales occur, such as a development at Double Bay. This will push up the average. Let's say in the next quarter a large number of low-cost rental accommodation in Campbelltown is completed and sold. Again, this will push the average down. The high-end properties have not reduced in value, thus you can never be sure that the short-term gains reported are achievable, or that the reductions equate to a buying opportunity. In my view, you can only be sure of long-term gains. My point also is that you cannot sit on the fence and wait for property to go down. History has proven that this will never happen. There might be bargains and distressed sales, but these are not the norm.

With market timing in mind, I asked Wilsons Advisory to do some projections for me based on a number of scenarios. I wanted to see what the long-term effect of being in the market would look like based on a simple investment strategy and linear projections.

The assumptions I used in the financial modelling are the following:

- The starting point is for a person who is 20 years old as at 1 July 2024. This could be any age, but I picked 20 as it is easy to compute. I then took five- and ten-year increments. This starting point could easily be 30.
- Household gross income (before tax) is $100,000 per annum. This may be the sole owner or a couple. This salary will increase by 3 per cent per annum, which is below the average salary increase over the past 20 years (which is 8.33%). The average weekly earnings over the past 40 years show 4.25 per cent growth. Of course, for a younger person whose career is blossoming, this average growth could be exceeded. Equally, if this is for a couple and one partner decides to reduce their work hours later in life to start a family, the above would be more than likely closer to reality.
- The tax payable on $100,000 is $24,967 (including 2% Medicare levy). For a couple, this would be less. It also assumes they have private health insurance, otherwise up

to an extra 1.75 per cent Medicare levy surcharge would be payable. For all future projections, I have used the tax rates applicable for the 2025 tax year, even though these may change in the future.

- The projections are based on the acquisition of five properties over a 16-year period, so one new property every four years. Rather than make this complicated, I showed every purchase at $1 million. Every additional property purchased is bought with 100 per cent gearing, using the increases in values of other property owned. Of course, in reality, the timing in certain markets may be quicker or slower.
- So as not to complicate the figures, I looked only at investment properties being purchased and not your (non-income earning) sole and principal residence. I purposely left this out as it, again, complicates the projections. The goal is to create a passive income portfolio.
- In the previous chapters, I stated that the first purchase is the hardest. This is where you need to save like crazy, get help and work two or three jobs just to break free.
- The first property is purchased 1 July 2024, being the start of the 2025 financial year ($1m cost, $800,000 loan) – assumes you have saved a $200,000 deposit (or obtained help, perhaps via a gift).
- The second property is purchased four years later, let's say on 1 July 2028 ($1m cost, $800,000 loan) – $200,000 deposit funded via drawdown/refinance from Loan #1. Hence, a total of $1 million loan.

- The third property is purchased 1 July 2032 ($1m cost, $800,000 loan) – $200,000 deposit funded via drawdown/refinance from Loans #1 and #2. Same as above total $1m loan.
- The fourth property is purchased 1 July 2036 ($1m cost, $800,000 loan) – $200,000 deposit funded via drawdown/refinance from Loans #1, 2 and 3.
- The fifth property is purchased 1 July 2040 ($1m cost, $800,000 loan) – $200,000 deposit funded via drawdown/refinance from Loans #1, 2, 3 and 4.

I have also assumed that the government will not make any changes to either negative gearing or the 50 per cent CGT discount. Prior to being elected it stated that it would not change either of the above. In fact the government has committed $10 billion to building 100,000 new homes.

As you can see, increases in property values assist with further acquisitions and allow these acquisitions to be 100 per cent geared. I have not factored in any principal reductions.

Property assumptions I used are the following:

- Growth 5 per cent per annum, a conservative number given property over the past 30 years has grown 5.4 per cent per annum.
- Income from rent is 3.5 per cent per annum of the property cost.
- Costs are 20 per cent of the rental income per annum.
- Depreciation $15,000 per annum of prime cost.

- Interest on loans is 6 per cent – they are interest-only loans and not principal and interest.
- Redraws to finance the deposits for properties #2–5 are at the above interest rates.

As stated earlier, I have used a person starting this journey at 20 years old for an easy number to work with. It could easily be 30, 40 or 50 years old.

The first property costs $1,000,000, with a loan of $800,000. Then every four years they buy another property and borrow the 20 per cent deposit. The table of costs is shown in Figure 2.

**Figure 2 Purchase cost and loan amount to create an investment property portfolio**

| Age | Cost | Loan |
|---|---:|---:|
| 20 | 1,000,000 | 800,000 |
| 24 | 1,000,000 | 1,000,000 |
| 28 | 1,000,000 | 1,000,000 |
| 32 | 1,000,000 | 1,000,000 |
| 36 | 1,000,000 | 1,000,000 |
| | 5,000,000 | 4,800,000 |

This person, at 36 or having followed this strategy for 16 years, has purchased $5 million of property and owes $4.8 million. This is because the last four properties are 100 per cent geared. On the face of it, this portfolio has a cost base of $5 million and a debt of $4.8 million. The original $200,000 deposit is the equity in the $5 million property portfolio (at cost).

At face value, this doesn't look that great, but we all know that the figures don't stop there. By purchasing one property every four years and with an average (linear) growth rate of 5 per cent per annum, after each five-year period the result in assets held is shown in Figure 3. The two columns are inflation-adjusted value in today's dollars and the future value in tomorrow's dollars – not inflation adjusted.

**Figure 3 Current value and future value of property portfolio**

| | Today's value $ | Future value $ |
|---|---|---|
| Starting journey – first purchase at age 20 | 1,000,000 | 1,000,000 |
| After 5 years, age 25 | 2,056,094 | 2,326,282 |
| After 10 years, age 30 | 3,180,642 | 4,071,490 |
| After 15 years, age 35 | 4,387,213 | 6,353,993 |
| After 20 years, age 40 | 5,690,771 | 9,324,990 |
| After 25 years, age 45 | 6,419,456 | 11,901,313 |
| After 30 years, age 50 | 7,241,448 | 15,189,427 |
| After 35 years, age 55 | 8,168,693 | 19,385,985 |
| After 40 years, age 60 | 9,214,669 | 24,741,975 |

It is staggering that in future dollars, this strategy could create a $24.7 million portfolio. Even in inflation-adjusted today's dollars, it would result in $9.2 million in assets (from a meagre $200,000 initial capital). If that doesn't make you realise the effect of being poor and sacrificing everything to save the initial $200,000 deposit, nothing will.

The only caveat that I must mention is that growth is not always linear. It will stay stagnant for a time, and then, without realising it, make massive jumps. This is why it is important to stay in the market.

Let me now turn my attention to income earned as an employee and then as an investor. Figure 4 illustrates how this person's income would grow as an employee, using the earlier projections.

**Figure 4 Income as adjusted for inflation both before and after tax**

| | Gross income | Tax payable | Net income after tax |
|---|---|---|---|
| Starting salary at age 20 | 100,000 | 24,967 | 75,033 |
| After 5 years, age 25 | 115,927 | 30,462 | 85,465 |
| After 10 years, age 30 | 134,392 | 37,480 | 96,912 |
| After 15 years, age 35 | 155,797 | 45,828 | 109,969 |
| After 20 years, age 40 | 180,611 | 55,554 | 125,057 |
| After 25 years, age 45 | 209,378 | 69,075 | 140,303 |
| After 30 years, age 50 | 242,726 | 84,749 | 157,977 |
| After 35 years, age 55 | 281,386 | 102,919 | 178,467 |
| After 40 years, age 60 | 326,204 | 123,983 | 202,221 |

I have assumed that the government will not make any adjustment to taxes to take into account bracket creep. In other words, tax will continue to rise as income increases. Bracket creep takes away some of your increases in income via additional taxes.

The other interesting point is that, after 40 years, this person will have a net income of $202,221, after adjusting for inflation. I would suggest that in 2064, this will not be enough income to live on, especially if the person did not, at least, own their own home. This is why those who do not have any savings or have not saved to create an investment portfolio will suffer a lifelong struggle to live on their wage alone.

Let me now add the income from rental properties purchased under the strategy discussed earlier. For ease of calculation, I have based rental income at 3.5 per cent of the property value.

**Figure 5 Consider now the employee receives rent from their property portfolio**

| | Salary | Rent | Total income | Expenses | Net income before dep'n |
|---|---|---|---|---|---|
| Starting position at age 20 | 100,000 | 35,000 | 135,000 | 55,000 | 80,000 |
| After 5 years, age 25 | 115,927 | 81,420 | 197,347 | 124,284 | 73,063 |
| After 10 years, age 30 | 134,392 | 142,502 | 276,894 | 196,500 | 80,394 |
| After 15 years, age 35 | 155,797 | 222,390 | 378,186 | 272,478 | 105,708 |
| After 20 years, age 40 | 180,611 | 326,375 | 506,986 | 353,275 | 153,711 |
| After 25 years, age 45 | 209,378 | 416,546 | 625,924 | 371,309 | 254,615 |
| After 30 years, age 50 | 242,726 | 531,631 | 774,356 | 394,326 | 380,030 |
| After 35 years, age 55 | 281,386 | 678,509 | 959,896 | 423,702 | 536,194 |
| After 40 years, age 60 | 326,204 | 865,970 | 1,192,173 | 461,194 | 730,979 |

It becomes clear that, after 40 years in the market, the rental income, which is passive income, on just five properties has way outstripped the salary income. In other words, this scenario clearly shows that at this stage, the person can give up working and still receive a substantial income ($865,970 gross per annum, or $404,776 net after expenses per annum).

It gets better. There are non-cash items like depreciation claims, plus expenses like interest, that are deductible against your salary income. In the early years, these additional tax claims subsidise your losses against your tax. This is how this investor is able to build their portfolio.

Figure 6 accounts for the taxation aspect and the net income after tax of this investment scenario.

**Figure 6 Taxation consequences of this investment strategy**

| | Net Income before dep'n | Depreciation | Taxable income | Tax payable | Net income after tax |
|---|---|---|---|---|---|
| Starting journey at age 20 | 80,000 | 15,000 | 65,000 | 12,892 | 52,108 |
| After 5 years, age 25 | 73,063 | 30,000 | 43,063 | 5,585 | 37,478 |
| After 10 years, age 30 | 80,394 | 45,000 | 35,394 | 3,975 | 31,419 |
| After 15 years, age 35 | 105,708 | 60,000 | 45,708 | 6,236 | 39,472 |
| After 20 years, age 40 | 153,711 | 75,000 | 78,711 | 17,622 | 61,089 |
| After 25 years, age 45 | 254,615 | 75,000 | 179,615 | 55,117 | 124,498 |
| After 30 years, age 50 | 380,030 | 75,000 | 305,030 | 114,032 | 190,998 |
| After 35 years, age 55 | 536,194 | 75,000 | 461,194 | 187,428 | 273,766 |
| After 40 years, age 60 | 730,979 | 75,000 | 655,979 | 278,977 | 377,002 |

Let's now pull this together. Figure 7 compares a person who did not embark on this journey with a person who followed the investment strategy, where the losses resulted in lower taxes being paid.

**Figure 7 Comparison: no property investment versus the investment strategy outlined**

| | Net income ($) no investment properties | Net income ($) five investment properties |
|---|---|---|
| Starting journey at age 20 | 76,212 | 52,108 |
| After 5 years, age 25 | 86,883 | 37,478 |
| After 10 years, age 30 | 99,254 | 31,419 |
| After 15 years, age 35 | 112,140 | 39,472 |
| After 20 years, age 40 | 127,029 | 61,089 |
| After 25 years, age 45 | 142,215 | 124,498 |
| After 30 years, age 50 | 159,473 | 190,998 |
| After 35 years, age 55 | 179,479 | 273,766 |
| After 40 years, age 60 | 202,672 | 377,002 |

The net income after tax and after all expenses has increased from $202,672 to $377,002. But the best part is that now this person has choices. With a property portfolio worth $24.7 million ($9.2 million in 2024 dollars), life has suddenly become easier.

Another aspect that is really interesting is the tax subsidy that occurs in the early years. If we consider the taxes payable for a person with rental properties over a 40-year period (as shown above), they are actually paying more tax in the later years. In the first 30 years, they save $147,980 in tax. In the last 20 years, they pay an extra $268,786 in tax. This is because now their income is higher. The ATO (through negative gearing subsidies) has helped this person create a massive property portfolio and the ATO will also reap the benefit from it in future years. This person has now created enough personal wealth to not be on social welfare of any kind, again saving the government money. Figure 8 shows the tax payable in the projected time period discussed.

**Figure 8 Comparison of taxes payable using this investment strategy versus doing nothing**

| | An investor with properties | A worker on a wage with no investment properties | Lower/higher tax payable |
|---|---|---|---|
| At age 20 | 12,892 | 24,967 | 12,075 |
| After 5 years, age 25 | 5,585 | 30,462 | 24,876 |
| After 10 years, age 30 | 3,975 | 37,480 | 33,505 |
| After 15 years, age 35 | 6,236 | 45,828 | 39,592 |
| After 20 years, age 40 | 17,622 | 55,554 | 37,932 |
| After 25 years, age 45 | 55,117 | 69,075 | 13,957 |
| After 30 years, age 50 | 114,032 | 84,749 | -29,283 |
| After 35 years, age 55 | 187,428 | 102,919 | -84,509 |
| After 40 years, age 60 | 278,977 | 123,983 | -154,994 |
| | 681,864 | 575,015 | -106,848 |

While certain lobby groups have been trying to persuade the government that negative gearing should be abolished, the above results clearly indicate that negative gearing provides more benefits than the cost to taxation would indicate. If the government tampers with negative gearing, it would more than likely require the quarantining of the early year losses (and the loss of the tax benefit). However, when in the later years the portfolio moves into making a profit, these prior year losses would be able to be used to offset future income. This would actually help the investor by reducing the future taxes payable. Hence any potential abolition of negative gearing will likely not be as bad as many think.

8

# Strategy for a 20- to 30-year-old investor

Chapter 7 highlighted how time in the market is so important; how mistakes made can, with time, smooth themselves out. In a person's lifetime property can double or triple in value. As mentioned earlier, it is not timing the market, but rather time in the market that is important. Also mentioned earlier, the median price of a house in Sydney in 1970 was $18,700; in December 2024, the medium was $1,627,625. This is an 870 per cent increase, an increase of 87 times the original cost in 53 years. Now consider that the average working life of a person is about 47 years. Imagine if, during this time, you accumulated property as per the scenario in the earlier chapter. At age 60, you have a property portfolio worth $24 million and a passive net income of $404,775 (Gross rent $865,970 – $461,194 Expenses).

We can all look back and see the opportunities missed. I mentioned an earlier situation when, in the 80s, my wife and I purchased a house at Earlwood in Sydney's inner west. We paid $26,000 for it. It was our home and, being a newly married, it was all we could afford. If only we had kept that property. I am sure it would be worth in excess of $1.5 million now. I am sure everyone will have experienced times in their life like this. My point is don't let these opportunities pass you by.

So, what is the strategy for a 20- to 30-year-old? I will assume the following will relate to this person or couple:

- They have just started their working life and hence their income may be a little low.
- They may be living at home or renting, may even be dating or just married.
- They will be spending all of their disposable income on living costs, including nights out with friends.
- They will be earning the average wage of $80,000 per annum; as a couple or with a side hustle, it may get to $100,000 per annum. On $80,000 per annum, the tax would be $16,467 and the after-tax income $63,612. On $100,000, the tax would be $24,967 and the net income $75,033.

At first glance, you might say they have no hope of buying their first home, whether that is an investment property or a place to live. But you would be wrong. I am not saying it would be easy – it will definitely be hard. There will be massive sacrifices and a total realignment of their spending habits and priorities. Frankly, the first step will always be the hardest, no matter what age a person is.

The things a person in this age group might consider to help themselves obtain the deposit they need to start their journey may be the following:

1. **Save like crazy.** This may mean forgoing those holidays, night club visits or other lifestyle things that will eat

up any spare capital that you have. Review some of the tips on breaking the poverty trap in Chapter 3. Apply whatever will work for you. The problem with this strategy is that we are experiencing a rising market at the moment and so the deposit amount is continuing to rise. Hence, the deposit gap is moving faster than normal savings may permit. It almost seems that, without some form of windfall or outside help, your first home purchase will keep moving away from you quicker than you can run towards it. If this is you, you need to consider the following additional options.

2. **Using the bank of Mum and Dad.** If you are lucky enough, you may be able to borrow or obtain help from your parents. This is extremely common for that first purchase. In fact, my father helped me with my first home with a gift to help with the deposit. Depending on your family situation, this assistance could be through a guarantee. For example, the loan you need may be at a high percentage to the value of the property, causing the bank to require additional security or guarantees to approve the loan. Alternatively, your parents could take a second mortgage on their home and lend that to you. If this path is taken, then your parents should have a lawyer prepare a loan document and even register a second mortgage on the property, behind the bank. Of course, there may be personal family considerations attached to this. If you have siblings, your parents may need to treat everyone fairly and equally. The other vital consideration is asset protection. I have seen many situations where the

parents have provided a guarantee and been forced to make good on that guarantee. This may be because the child they lent the money to or allowed a second mortgage on their home for has experienced an unfortunate event, leading to the necessity to sell the property at a loss. In some cases, the above distressed sale may arise from a divorce or family breakdown. The other problem I have seen happen is that a child goes into business with rose-coloured glasses on and loses everything, necessitating bankruptcy. Therefore, we would also recommend that the parent who provides this type of assistance take a second mortgage to cover themselves. At least they should have a loan document drawn up which can be secured via a caveat on a title. If your parents have concerns about providing loans or guarantees, they could become joint tenants with you on this purchase. Of course, all tax deductions will only be available to both in proportion to the ownership structure.

3. **Consider purchasing your first property with a friend or relative.** In this case, the property could be purchased as joint tenants, with both parties each owning 50 per cent. That way each person only needs to help cover half the deposit. As they only need half the deposit, this may be easier. Of course, they are only acquiring half of their first property. If this path is chosen, I would recommend that a partnership agreement be entered into to ensure both parties are equally commit to all costs and, if one party decides to sell, the other party has the first option to acquire the other person's share. I would also recommend

that the agreement locks both parties into the property for an initial defined period of time and that, in this initial period, both parties must agree to sell. If they both don't agree, the property will not be sold. This helps cover any short-term sale that may not be in the best interests of both parties. As mentioned earlier, you need to hold property for as long as possible to make gains.

4. **Consider the First Home Super Saver (FHSS) scheme.** This scheme, introduced by the government, allows first home buyers to save their first deposit inside the super fund and then withdraw that money before they are eligible to retire. Because superannuation is concessionally taxed (at only 15 per cent), the FHSS scheme should allow you to save money faster for a deposit on your first home. You can make additional voluntary salary-sacrificed superannuation contributions up to $15,000 per year (and $50,000 in total) into your complying superannuation fund, which can be withdrawn to help finance a deposit on your first home. You can use the scheme if you are a first home buyer and you satisfy both of the following tests:
   - You occupy the premises you purchase or intend to occupy it as soon as practicable, and
   - You intend to occupy the property for at least six months within the first 12 months you own it, after it is practical to move in.

Various other eligibility conditions must be satisfied. From 20 September 2024, changes were made to make this scheme more flexible. Some of these changes are retrospective to 1 July 2018. If you are considering this scheme, make sure you comply with all of the rules. The FHSS scheme is primarily aimed at low- to middle-income earners acquiring their first home. It does not apply to investment properties purchased. You could buy your first home, live in it until you meet the qualifying period, then move out and rent it.

5. **Help to Buy Scheme.** This is an Australian Government scheme to make it easier for low- to middle-income earners to buy their first home. It has limited places and allows a deposit of 5 per cent with a government guarantee of 15 per cent. The balance must be borrowed via an approved participating lender. The scheme is administered by Housing Australia.

   Whatever it takes, first home buyers should take advantage of every incentive ranging from reduced stamp duty to 5 per cent mortgage deposits. Even if that means living in the property for the qualifying period, they should do it.

My point is that when you are young, you have so much time on your side to really grow a massive property portfolio. You need to find a way to get onto that first rung of the ladder, hence my comments to beg and borrow to do whatever it takes to obtain the initial deposit for your first step on this journey.

You may need to forgo many of the things young people get caught up in – going out with friends, spending money at nightclubs, buying a new car with a loan – but your focus must be on saving that initial $100,000 to $200,000 deposit.

Following this strategy over time results in a $24.7 million portfolio with a $4.8 million debt. Forgo a few pleasures early in life to reap massive rewards for your future.

Read and re-read the chapter on the ten tips to break the poverty trap. I guarantee you that if you can sacrifice whatever it takes to acquire your first property during this 20- to 30-year age bracket and you manage to keep it and build on it, you will never look back. You will be a person that others will say is 'lucky', but in reality, you know you just worked hard and sacrificed to get started. Like a snowball rolling down a hill, the momentum will create a wealth scenario that will be the envy of your friends that chose the nightclub life over savings. By the time you reach retirement, two or three massive property cycles will have happened, and you will be sitting on ten or more investment properties and a passive income that others will envy.

## Choosing growth or cash flow for your first property

It is so important that you do your own research. Don't be led by others that may or may not know what is right for you. When you are looking to buy, there are many alternatives and options, which could leave your head spinning and even lead to procrastination. For example, do you buy off the plan, do you buy new or second-hand, do you buy a unit or house, do you buy in a built-up area, do you buy in a regional area or a capital city?

For your first investment property, forget all of the above. If you are in your early working life, your income may be a little low, so negative gearing and tax saving are not vital. You are young, so initial growth is not that vital because you have lots of time in the market. What you really want is strong cash flow. You must look for a property that will give you a rent return over and above your financial commitments. It must yield at least 9–11 per cent return but still be in a good area. You might say that this is impossible, but it is not. This is why research is so important.

The other thing to look for is mortgagee or council foreclosures. Often, banks will simply want out. Talk to real estate agents in areas where the initial price may be affordable. Be ready to buy a bargain and tell the agents that you are ready if a distressed sale comes up. Sometimes a divorce or similar event makes people need to sell quickly. Scan the real estate websites, as these situations do come up all the time. Be alert to something that may need a bit of work, such as a repaint, or something that others avoid because it is messy or hard to visualise what it could look like once cleaned up. Don't be in a hurry for your first property, but don't sit on your hands either.

I recall the time a friend had a unit at Marsfield in Sydney. He was looking to start a family and the only place he could find that was within his budget was at Berowra, just north of Sydney. The price was, from memory, about $90,000 for a large block and an old 1960s fibro house. He could almost meet the deposit and loan amount. He borrowed extra on his credit card and he borrowed from friends, but he got there. At the same time, I purchased a new Mercedes Sports for the same money. Needless to say, that house tripled in value over the next five years. My car halved in value in the next ten years, plus I incurred high interest costs.

Resist buying a new car that may require a loan. Resist committing to spending all of your after-tax income and resist building up credit card debt that will affect any future bank loans.

Take on any side hustles to improve your income (Airtasker, etc). Stay home at night and save like your future depends on it, because it will. These early life decisions and priorities will be what will differentiate you from others in ten to 20 years' time.

Create your initial deposit, go to your bank or broker and get a loan approval by whatever way you can. Be flexible on where you look but be ready to act. In today's market, it is a seller's market, but this won't always be the case. Interest rates have risen and are now beginning to fall but it will take time for the effect of these falls to have any impact on the market. For many people, the damage of high interest rates and increased cost of living has already been done and there will be distressed sales. There will always be bargains or situations that will meet these criteria, or a case that luck is created when preparedness and opportunity meet. Do your research, be prepared and act quickly when you find something that meets your criteria and you can afford it (even if you need to stretch a little).

We all know that the projections in Chapter 7 are just that: estimates of the future. But my advice for a person in this age bracket is to follow your dreams. Use this strategy to build a passive income portfolio. Those that have done this have continued to move on with further purchases. The five properties listed are simply examples of a strategy. A person at this point in their life, once they achieve the first few properties, will be able to keep going. Many that have done that own more than 20 properties. Robert Kiyosaki is reported to own 15,000 investment properties. Managing that is a business in itself.

9

# Strategy for a 30- to 40-year-old investor

Generally, this is the time that most people start to think about their retirement nest egg. They may think about it, but often don't take action. Retirement is still over 20 years away and today's problems are top of mind. Typically, they will have purchased their first home and will be struggling with school fees and keeping up with their lifestyle choices. Their income will be starting to rise, but so will tax. They will be always complaining that they never have enough to cover their bills, complain about taxation but still want that new car. Because of interest rate increases over the past couple of years, the situation could be worse.

If that describes your situation, what is the answer? Well, you may not like it, but you need to break free of the poverty trap. You may even disagree that you are heading into a poverty trap. Believe me, you are. This is particularly true as you get older and retirement income is an issue. This is also true if a major life event happens, like you lose your job or have an accident. Make some serious changes to your income and spending. Remember what Albert Einstein said: doing the same thing over and over again is a sign of insanity. I will not pretend it will be easy, but you must break the cycle; otherwise, you will never become financially free.

The first step is to really look hard at your income. That may sound crazy, but there are two factors at play here that will cause you to be trapped: either not enough income, or expenses are too high. Look at both and make corrections. Investigate things like the following:

- Can I supplement my income with some form of side hustle?
- If married, can we both work and hence improve our income?
- Can we move back in with our in-laws to save rent or rent out our house?
- Looking at your current job, are you being rewarded sufficiently? Can you upskill yourself to increase your worth and income?
- On the expenses side, be really serious about your costs. Should you downsize your car, or stop any wasteful habits like smoking, gambling or going out to dinner?

I know the above sounds harsh and may take the fun out of living, but remember the big picture. You have 20 to 25 years left in your working life, to accumulate an asset level sufficient to give you the financial freedom you want (or need). There may only be one or two big property cycles left. If you are careful now, you will achieve it. Time will be your biggest ally to achieving this, so don't let it be your enemy by leaving things too late.

Let's discuss the strategy. Your income at this stage of life should be starting to grow and be at a reasonable level. You will be contributing a large percentage to the taxation office, possibly about 30–40 per cent of your pre-tax dollars, and you are probably complaining about that. The worst part is that the tax office never sends you a 'thank you' card. They even have the audacity to charge you interest if you are late in paying a 'pay as you go' tax instalment. While the steps listed are needed to create a small savings nest egg, a key part of the strategy is to use the tax saving on your high income to give your financial journey to freedom a boost. But I cannot stress enough that you need some of your own money to start the journey (for a deposit). You could 100 per cent gear an investment, but that is risky, particularly as the current property market may be at a current peak and will need time to reach the next peak.

## Financial modelling and reasoning

If we use the table in the earlier chapter and pick a person at 30 years of age, we can model a similar scenario. As an employee, using the projections below, this person's income has grown as shown below:

**Figure 9 Income and taxes payable in 30- to 40-year-old age bracket, according to wage increase projections**

| | Salary | Tax payable | Medicare levy | Total tax payable | Net income after tax |
|---|---|---|---|---|---|
| Starting salary at age 30 | 180,000 | 51,667 | 3,600 | 55,267 | 124,733 |
| After 5 years, age 35 | 208,669 | 64,568 | 4,173 | 68,741 | 139,928 |
| After 10 years, age 40 | 241,905 | 79,524 | 4,838 | 84,362 | 157,543 |
| After 15 years, age 45 | 280,434 | 96,862 | 5,609 | 102,471 | 177,963 |
| After 20 years, age 50 | 325,100 | 116,962 | 6,502 | 123,464 | 201,636 |
| After 25 years, age 55 | 376,880 | 140,263 | 7,538 | 147,801 | 229,079 |
| After 30 years, age 60 | 436,907 | 167,275 | 8,738 | 176,013 | 260,894 |
| After 35 years, age 65 | 506,495 | 198,590 | 10,130 | 208,720 | 297,775 |

These taxes are based on the 2025 tax rates and tax payable as the income rises into the next tax brackets. The Medicare levy is based on 2 per cent and is payable by all Australian taxpayers, with very few exceptions. It assumes the person has private health insurance and hence does not pay the Medicare levy surcharge, which can be as high at 1.5 per cent of taxable income.

The other interesting point is that this person, after 35 years and after adjusting for inflation, will have a net income of $297,775. If you do not own your own home, this will be difficult to live on, especially at this stage in your life with a family, school fees and the general pressures of life.

Let's now add the net income from rental properties purchased under the scenarios discussed in earlier chapters. For ease of calculation, I have based rental income at 3.5 per cent of the property value.

**Figure 10 Net income including rental properties**

| | Salary | Rent income | Total income | Expenses | Net income before dep'n |
|---|---|---|---|---|---|
| Starting salary at age 30 | 180,000 | 35,000 | 215,000 | 55,000 | 160,000 |
| After 5 years, age 35 | 208,669 | 81,420 | 290,089 | 124,284 | 165,805 |
| After 10 years, age 40 | 241,905 | 142,502 | 384,407 | 196,500 | 187,907 |
| After 15 years, age 45 | 280,434 | 222,390 | 502,824 | 272,478 | 230,346 |
| After 20 years, age 50 | 325,100 | 326,375 | 651,475 | 353,275 | 298,200 |
| After 25 years, age 55 | 376,880 | 416,546 | 793,426 | 371,309 | 422,117 |
| After 30 years, age 60 | 436,907 | 531,630 | 968,537 | 394,326 | 574,211 |
| After 35 years, age 65 | 506,495 | 678,509 | 1,185,004 | 423,702 | 761,302 |

Even after 30 years in the market, the rent income, which is passive income, on just five properties has way outstripped the salary income. In other words, this scenario clearly shows that at this stage, the person can give up working at age 65 and still receive a substantial income ($678,509 gross per annum or $254,807 net after expenses per annum).

As mentioned earlier, there are non-cash items, like depreciation claims, that are deductible against your salary income, allowing you to build your portfolio.

Figure 11 brings to account the taxation aspect of this investment scenario. It assumes that the government hasn't changed the rules to allow a person to offset property losses to other income and hence obtain the tax relief noted below.

**Figure 11 Taxation implications for this investment strategy**

| | Net income before dep'n | Dep'n | Net income | Income tax payable | Net income after tax |
|---|---|---|---|---|---|
| Starting salary at age 30 | 160,000 | 15,000 | 145,000 | 41,617 | 103,383 |
| After 5 years, age 35 | 165,805 | 30,000 | 135,805 | 38,031 | 97,774 |
| After 10 years, age 40 | 187,907 | 45,000 | 142,907 | 40,801 | 102,106 |
| After 15 years, age 45 | 230,346 | 60,000 | 170,346 | 51,502 | 118,844 |
| After 20 years, age 50 | 298,200 | 75,000 | 223,200 | 75,571 | 147,629 |
| After 25 years, age 55 | 422,117 | 75,000 | 347,117 | 133,812 | 213,305 |
| After 30 years, age 60 | 574,211 | 75,000 | 499,211 | 205,296 | 293,915 |
| After 35 years, age 65 | 761,302 | 75,000 | 686,302 | 293,229 | 393,073 |

Now, let's pull this together. Let us compare if this person did not embark on this journey, but only earned their income each year and paid tax accordingly to the scenario where the person purchased properties, earned rent, paid interest and built a passive income portfolio. We'll look at the cash flow effect, which adds back depreciation, as this is a non-cash flow item that simply allows a tax write-off. Hence, I have added back the depreciation to the net income earned by the property investor.

**Figure 12 Comparison: investment versus no investment**

| | Net income after tax, no investment properties | Net income after tax with 5 investment properties |
|---|---|---|
| Starting salary at age 30 | 124,733 | 118,383 |
| After 5 years, age 35 | 139,928 | 127,774 |
| After 10 years, age 40 | 157,543 | 147,106 |
| After 15 years, age 45 | 177,963 | 178,844 |
| After 20 years, age 50 | 201,636 | 222,629 |
| After 25 years, age 55 | 229,079 | 288,305 |
| After 30 years, age 60 | 260,894 | 368,915 |
| After 35 years, age 65 | 297,775 | 468,073 |

The net income using the investment strategy, after tax and after all expenses, has increased from $297,775 to $468,073 (57%). If they decided to give up working at age 65, they would have a gross passive income of $678,509 (expenses and tax would be payable, of course). They could choose to sell down to repay debt or even purchase more properties to increase their income and, with clever planning, reduce their tax. With a property portfolio worth $24.7 million ($9.2 million in 2024 dollars), life has suddenly become easier. But the best part is that now this person has choices. They no longer need to work for a living, having built a passive income portfolio.

I know the sacrifices in the early part of this journey may have been hard, but the above shows they are worth it.

10

# Strategy for a 40- to 50+-year-old investor

Many may say that once over 50, you are too old to begin this journey. While there may be some limitations, the bottom line is that you are never too old to commence a journey to financial freedom. You just need to work a little harder and maybe for longer. Retirement age is no longer set in stone at 65. Most people need or want to keep working, sometimes for financial reasons and sometimes because they love what they do. Working gives a purpose in life, a reason to get up in the morning. At 50 years of age, let's assume you have 20 years working life left. This is more than enough time to boost your retirement nest egg. There may be one or two property cycles left, depending on luck and timing. No one ever knows when property will stay level or boom.

Let's call this period your twilight years, a time when life is good, when your income (and tax payable) will be high and your living expenses will be starting to diminish. At age 40, this may not exactly be the case, but at age 50 this should start to occur. Your children may have left school, your mortgage will be a lot less and your income higher. Of course, you will be complaining about paying too much tax, as Figure 13 will confirm.

**Figure 13 Income projections and taxes payable**

| | Salary | Total tax payable | Net income after tax |
|---|---|---|---|
| Starting salary at age 40 | 200,000 | 51,938 | 148,062 |
| After 5 years, age 45 | 231,855 | 64,676 | 167,179 |
| After 10 years, age 50 | 268,783 | 80,371 | 188,412 |
| After 15 years, age 55 | 311,593 | 98,565 | 213,028 |
| After 20 years, age 60 | 361,222 | 119,657 | 241,565 |
| After 25 years, age 65 | 418,756 | 144,109 | 274,647 |
| After 30 years, age 70 | 485,452 | 211,291 | 274,161 |

From a tax and investment point of view, I have listed strategies to maximise your wealth in the time left. From Figure 13, we can see that tax is really biting into your after-tax dollars. It is hard to save for retirement when almost 50 per cent of your income leaves you before you receive it. It assumes that the government hasn't changed the rules to allow a person to offset property losses to other income and hence obtain the tax relief noted below. Therefore, the following are strategies to consider:

1. Increase your balances into tax-effective areas. By this, I mean reducing, with a matter of urgency, all non-deductible debt. For example, if you have an investment property that is almost paid off (and this may sound extreme), consider selling the property and buying another. The sale proceeds should be used to pay any debt remaining on your home loan. The new property will be geared to whatever balance needed to acquire it (100%, if necessary). You need to consider any capital gains tax payable, but this will help turn non-tax deductible debt into tax deductible debt. The following superannuation strategy might help mitigate any CGT payable.

2. Increase the amounts in superannuation. Superannuation is a tax-free environment when in pension mode and tax advantaged (15% only) in accumulation mode. The goal now will be to maximise your superannuation balances to the full extent allowable, based on your age and the various caps. This may involve:
   - Using the downsizer rules if you sell your sole and principal residence, providing you have owned it for 10 years and are 55 years of age or older (but under 75). The downsizer contribution allows an extra $300,000 ($600,000 for couples) to be contributed. It is a non-concessional contribution and so not tax deductible. It is also not subject to any annual non-concessional caps.
   - You could also use the downsizer rules to release the equity in your home by selling it and investing some of the proceeds into superannuation as above. You could use a small part of the proceeds to build a granny flat at the rear of your children's home. Or of course you could purchase a smaller home.
   - If you haven't used all of your concessional contributions cap, you can catch up any used amounts for any or all of the prior five years. This contribution will be tax deductible. For 2025, the concessional cap is $30,000 per annum. For earlier years, it was $27,500. This catch-up will give you a one-off tax deduction.
   - Use the non-concessional caps to get more money into super. If you have investments outside of super, why pay half of the income you earn to the ATO?

Consider a strategy to move these assets (or the cash) into super. There is a bring forward rule that allows up to three years of non-concessional caps to be paid in a year. The current cap is $120,000. A good strategy of how to maximise this is to pay $120,000 in, say, June 2025. Then in July 2025 use the bring forward rule to pay the 2026, 2027 and 2028 cap, a total of $360,000. Together with the earlier $120,000, this will make an extra $480,000 moved into super. If you are a couple, this figure would be $960,000.

- When you reach a condition of release and your super moves into pension mode, you must withdraw an age-based pension from your fund. But the part many do not realise is this age-based pension is tax free. The income earned by the fund is tax free and the amount you draw as a pension is tax free.

**Figure 14 Age-based minimum pension withdrawal**

| Age on 1 July or, if commenced in the financial year, the commencement date | Minimum %* of account balance you must withdraw each year |
|---|---|
| Under 65 | 4% |
| 65 to 74 | 5% |
| 75 to 79 | 6% |
| 80 to 84 | 7% |
| 85 to 89 | 9% |
| 90 to 94 | 11% |
| 95+ | 14% |

*Based on the balance held by the member as at the prior 1 July each year. For the 2025 tax year, the above minimum pension withdrawal amount is calculated based on the balance at 1 July 2024. There is no maximum withdrawal. You can (but why would you?) withdraw your full pension balance.

- Within your fund, each member (if a couple) can have a notional pension account and an accumulation account. Income and profit is apportioned on these balances. The pension account portion of income is tax free, while the accumulation portion is taxed at 15 per cent. Contributions into the fund must go into the accumulation account. This is because the rules state a pension cannot be added to. However, you can commute (transfer) a pension balance back to accumulation, pick up any balance in the accumulation account and then roll the new balance into a new pension account. For example, assume your accumulation balance is $250,000 and pension balance $500,000, give a total $750,000. The income of the fund will be apportioned, hence only 33 per cent on the net income will be taxed at 15 per cent. However, if on 1 July the pension balance of $500,000 is commuted back to accumulation and a new pension of $750,000 is established, no tax will be payable on the new pension balance of $750,000. This is an important strategy that many fail to do. It is actually a very simple step. Also, if the members reach preservation age (meet a condition of release), the fund should immediately be moved into pension mode. This will ensure the tax-free status of all income including capital gains.
- Superannuation is a complex area due to the tax incentives available. There are restrictions based on age, the balance held and the taxable/non-taxable

> components. You will need to obtain advice on the strategies discussed to ensure you comply with all of the superannuation rules. These can be onerous, but if you use the benefits, the saving can be a very important part of your wealth creation journey.

Personally, I am a big fan of super, for the reasons mentioned, but it helps that I hold a Chartered Accountant SMSF Specialist qualification with Chartered Accountants Australia and New Zealand. Now that you are in your twilight years, you need to use this tax haven to the max. With superannuation, it can be managed by others (a public, retail or wholesale fund) or self-managed. You would use a public fund if you didn't want the hassle of managing it yourself. The rules for both are the same. However, if you wanted to own some of your investment properties in super, you must use a self-managed super fund. Personally, I hold some property in super, but the majority of my self-managed super fund assets are shares or managed funds. I hold shares that are listed on both the Australian and overseas exchanges. I do this because, firstly, I want to diversify my investments. I do not want all of my retirement nest egg in one basket. Secondly, Australian shares give me franking credits, which are fully refundable. When I lodge my super fund tax return, I actually get a large tax refund. And thirdly, the income I withdraw is tax free. I use financial advisors to manage my fund, as frankly I have never been good at picking the share market, so I leave that to the experts.

While it might sound obvious that you have the option to acquire assets (properties, shares or managed funds) either in your own name or in your super fund, you now need to decide which will be the best option for you. If you are over 50, superannuation must be an important part of any decision-making process. In less than 15 years (subject to the preservation rules), you will be able to move your member balance into pension mode. The properties in your super fund should be debt free, as the tax deduction for interest is only minimal (15% in accumulation mode, 0% in pension mode). In super, capital gains tax is 10 per cent in accumulation mode and zero in pension mode.

In earlier chapters, I covered the various entities that property should be purchased in. Now that your income is high, you may wish to consider any highly geared properties be purchased in your own name and ungeared property be purchased in your super fund. My key point is to now think very laterally about this. Take charge, make intelligent decisions that are right for you and achieve your goals of a passive income portfolio.

An easy way to consider a few alternatives available might be to consider a hypothetical example of Mr Black and Mrs White. The options at this twilight age are endless, as everyone will have different situations that may apply, so there may be many shades of grey between Mr Black and Mrs White. But this will give you some idea of what might apply to your situation and what is possible.

## Mr Black

Mr Black has a home in Sydney with a value of $2 million. His mortgage is $800,000 and he earns an income of $200,000 per annum. He has some super in an industry fund, but sees his house as his primary asset for future wealth creation. This would be a typical situation for the average person. He has no income left each week and struggles at times to pay for any luxuries in life, especially the designer handbags his partner may want. Figure 15 illustrates what his short balance sheet and income statement could look like. It doesn't take account of cars or consumable items.

**Figure 15 Balance sheet and income statement for Mr Black**

| Item | $ |
|---|---|
| Home | 2,000,000 |
| Mortgage | 800,000 |
| Net equity | 1,200,000 |
| Gross income | 200,000 |
| Tax payable | 51,938 |
| Net income after tax | 148,062 |
| Less home loan interest (say, 6%) | 48,000 |
| Net disposal income | 100,062 |

He has $100,062 after tax for living expenses, holidays, car expenses and all the usual costs associated with living in Sydney. He may also be required by his bank to make principal repayments. These extra principal repayments could be another $20,000 per annum. With car repayments, his disposable income could be less than $1000 per week. Let's examine this in detail and where this strategy will take him.

His income projections could be as noted in Figure 16:

**Figure 16 Mr Black's possible income projections**

| | Salary | Total tax payable | Net income after tax |
|---|---|---|---|
| Starting salary at age 50 | 200,000 | 64,667 | 135,333 |
| After 5 years, age 55 | 231,855 | 79,639 | 152,216 |
| After 10 years, age 60 | 268,783 | 96,995 | 171,788 |
| After 15 years, age 65 | 311,593 | 117,116 | 194,477 |
| After 20 years, age 70 | 361,222 | 140,441 | 220,781 |
| After 25 years, age 75 | 418,756 | 167,482 | 251,274 |

If Mr Black does nothing, at age 75 his net income (after tax) will be $251,274, but he cannot work forever so that will soon cease. His house in 2024 is worth $2 million; in 2054, based on a 3.5 per cent growth rate, his property will be worth around $7.2 million in 2024 dollars. However, this will be the mean price of houses in Sydney in 2054, so he will not have any surplus funds. He is okay, but nowhere near the net worth of those that follow the investment property path. He will have some superannuation, but this will be hard to gauge as it will depend on how long he has been employed. But will he have a sufficient income to live on without some form of aid, like a government pension? It is highly unlikely.

## Mrs White

Let's now look at the radical Mrs White. She decides it is time to take some drastic action. She wants to spread her investments and create an investment portfolio. She recognises that she needs to use her money better and needs to think about the tax side.

**Figure 17 Mrs White's radical plan**

| Item | $ |
|---|---|
| Sells home – proceeds | 2,000,000 |
| Repays mortgage | 800,000 |
| Net proceeds | 1,200,000 |
| | |
| Buy new home (no debt) | 1,000,000 |
| Keeps for extra super contributions later but initially places into an offset account for security | 200,000 |
| Buys investment property 1 | 1,000,000 |
| Borrows | 1,000,000 |

With the offset account she pays interest only on $800,000 at, say, 6.5 per cent.

The assumptions are the following:

1. She sells her home for $2 million and buys a new home for $1 million. I know that may sound radical and a step backwards, but she needs to spread her investments and not have all of her eggs in the one basket. Her new home will be debt free.
2. She purchases her first investment property for $1 million.
3. She borrows $1 million for the property purchase, but places $200,000 into an offset account. This will reduce the interest on the $1 million. The offset account will give her some security if things go wrong, such as losing her job. It can also be used for additional contributions into super if in one year her tax bill is a little high.

She now monitors the property growth and, if and when opportunities arise or bargains present themselves, she can begin an acquisition strategy.

The plan will be to buy one property every four to five years, as shown in Figure 18. Mrs White needs to be careful and buy well. She needs to do her research and only buy quality assets, as noted earlier in the book. In other words, she cannot blindly follow a strategy. But she cannot sit on the fence and do nothing either. She must act. The assumed acquisitions are shown below:

**Figure 18 Assumed acquisition strategy for Mrs White**

| Age | Cost | Loan |
|---|---|---|
| Age 50 | 1,000,000 | 800,000 |
| Age 55 | 1,000,000 | 1,000,000 |
| Age 60 | 1,000,000 | 1,000,000 |
| Age 65 | 1,000,000 | 1,000,000 |

What does this look like, asset wise, at age 65? Mrs White has acquired four investment properties, all 100 per cent geared with corresponding tax write-offs. I stress that these projections are linear projections. In reality, markets may average a growth rate higher or lower in any period. History tells us that the average will be approximately 5.4 per cent, projected below:

**Figure 19 Market growth based on historical averages**

| Age | Today's value | Future value |
|---|---|---|
| At age 50 | 1,000,000 | 1,000,000 |
| After 5 years, age 55 | 2,056,094 | 2,326,282 |
| After 10 years, age 60 | 3,180,642 | 4,071,491 |
| After 15 years, age 65 | 4,387,213 | 6,353,992 |
| After 20 years, age 70 | 4,475,265 | 8,109,484 |
| After 25 years, age 75 | 6,419,456 | 10,349,985 |

If Mrs White decides to retire at age 70, her portfolio in 2044 dollars will be worth $8,109,484 with a debt of $4 million. By only using the bank's money (not her own), she has accumulated over $4 million in net worth. If we continue the above to age 75, the portfolio is worth $10,349,985 (over $6m in net worth). But at age 70, Mrs White now has choices. She might consider other alternatives, such as selling down some of her assets. Of course, her home will have also increased in value, but she needs to ignore that because she needs somewhere to live.

Let's now look at Mrs White's income to age 75, which will include rent received and interest paid on her loans. Again, these are projections only based on linear growth rates for salary and rent increases.

**Figure 20 Mrs White's projected income**

| | Salary | Rent income | Total income | Expenses | Net income before dep'n |
|---|---|---|---|---|---|
| At age 50 | 200,000 | 35,000 | 235,000 | 55,000 | 180,000 |
| After 5 years, age 55 | 231,855 | 81,420 | 313,275 | 124,284 | 188,991 |
| After 10 years, age 60 | 268,783 | 142,502 | 411,285 | 196,501 | 214,784 |
| After 15 years, age 65 | 311,593 | 222,390 | 533,983 | 272,477 | 261,506 |
| After 20 years, age 70 | 361,222 | 283,832 | 645,054 | 296,766 | 348,288 |
| After 25 years, age 75 | 418,756 | 362,250 | 781,006 | 312,450 | 468,556 |

Mrs White is now earning a gross income of $781,006, before interest and other rental expenses. It can easily be seen that once Mrs White needs to stop working, and perhaps sells one of her properties to reduce debt, she has the ability to earn substantial passive income. At this stage, she has four rental properties worth $8.1 million at age 70 or $10.3 million at age 75 and owes $4 million to the bank, assuming the initial $200,000 in her offset account has been placed into superannuation.

If we take this strategy a step further and consider Mrs White's non-cash depreciation and expense claims, such as interest and rental property costs, Mrs White will earn, after tax, the net income shown below:

**Figure 21 Mrs White's projected after-tax net income**

| | Net income before dep'n | Dep'n | Net income | Total tax payable | Net income after tax |
|---|---|---|---|---|---|
| At age 50 | 180,000 | 15,000 | 165,000 | 49,417 | 115,583 |
| After 5 years, age 55 | 188,991 | 30,000 | 158,991 | 47,074 | 111,917 |
| After 10 years, age 60 | 214,784 | 45,000 | 169,784 | 51,283 | 118,501 |
| After 15 years, age 65 | 261,506 | 60,000 | 201,506 | 65,375 | 136,131 |
| After 20 years, age 70 | 348,288 | 75,000 | 273,288 | 99,113 | 174,175 |
| After 25 years, age 75 | 468,556 | 75,000 | 393,556 | 155,638 | 237,918 |

If we add back the non-cash aspect of depreciation claimed, Mrs White's true after-tax income is shown in Figure 22. At age 75, she has $312,918 in income, after tax.

**Figure 22 Mrs White's income up to age 75, after tax**

| | Net income | Total tax payable | Net income after tax | Dep'n | Net income excluding dep'n |
|---|---|---|---|---|---|
| At Age 50 | 165,000 | 49,417 | 115,583 | 15,000 | 130,583 |
| After 5 years, age 55 | 158,991 | 47,074 | 111,917 | 30,000 | 141,917 |
| After 10 years, age 60 | 169,784 | 51,283 | 118,501 | 45,000 | 163,501 |
| After 15 years, age 65 | 201,506 | 65,375 | 136,131 | 60,000 | 196,131 |
| After 20 years, age 70 | 273,288 | 99,113 | 174,175 | 75,000 | 249,175 |
| After 25 years, age 75 | 393,556 | 155,638 | 237,918 | 75,000 | 312,918 |

Mrs White's net income after tax is $312,918. If you look back at Mr Black's situation, his after-tax income at age 75 is $251,274. You can see a slight improvement. But the difference is Mrs White now has a property portfolio worth $10.3 million, plus she owns her own home outright, no mortgage. Mrs White is now no longer dependent on anyone for her future retirement needs.

This is, of course, a simple projection of what might occur in these two scenarios. There are many shades of grey between what Mrs White and Mr Black could do, given their situation and age.

This is only an example of what is possible and the future effect of these decisions. It also assumes the government has not changed the rules on negative gearing. Although, even if it did, the result will not change, only the extra tax benefits in the early stages of this journey. Even though Mrs White begins this journey at 50 years of age, she now has choices on selling down her properties, transferring money to superannuation or even simply helping her children with any of their needs. Mr Black has taken a conservative path that will not yield the future gains that Mrs White will earn. For Mrs White, she will be set up financially in her retirement years with enough assets and income to more than cover her needs.

11

# Negative gearing – how to use it

Most people understand negative gearing, but just in case, let me explain it as simply as possible. Then I will explain how to use it to your advantage.

In the previous chapters, I have shown how, when you embark on a journey of property acquisitions, taxation can give you the help you need to actually achieve your objectives. At the end of Chapter 7, the taxation projections show that a person in the first stage of this wealth creation journey actually saves $147,980 in tax (assuming the government hasn't changed negative gearing). In the later stages, as their income increases, they pay more tax, but that is okay.

What is important is that it will give you a chance to get started. The tax saved, or the tax refunded, will help you cover those initial property purchases that may be a little beyond achieving. In other words, this will give you a boost.

I will cover how this works and why without it certain sectors of the economy (such as employees or those on fixed incomes) cannot build wealth any other way. In Australia, teachers, nurses, truckies and police force employees are among the country's largest groups of property investors.

Negative gearing can provide a helping hand when you start out but, as you will see in the case studies, as your profits and gains increase, it will no longer be relevant. The ability to gain a tax deduction on the interest paid on loans is a way to use bank money to make more money and use the tax deductibility of the interest to help reduce your tax.

The investment you consider must stack up. Do not enter into a loan for tax reasons only. Do not spend $1 to save 47 cents. That would not make economic sense. Also, be aware that leverage and gearing only work if the asset increases in value. If it goes down, then the loss is increased by the gearing ratio. You would invest if you knew that the $1 expenditure would earn you a return of, say, 15 per cent and, in time, be worth $2. That would make sense.

For the purpose of this exercise, I will cover the tax aspects, noting that these assumptions are a given and that the investment must make economic sense. Always do your research.

Assume you buy a business, rental property, share portfolio or commercial investment. The formula holds true no matter what the underlying asset is. Let's say, for example, that you purchase an asset for $1 million that you know is undervalued and that you can make money on. You must do your homework on this. Don't take any short cuts or go into the transaction based on a well-oiled salesman's hype. In other words, remove any rose-coloured glasses. You have completed your homework and you are as confident as you can be that the asset being purchased is an income-producing asset, even if, at this stage, it will take a year or two to provide a reasonable rent return. If you borrowed 100 per cent on the purchase price at 6 per cent interest, you have an immediate write-off of $60,000. If you have income from other areas (like your salary), then this $60,000 write-off (interest only) could be worth $28,200 in reduced tax or as a tax refund. Assume you capitalise the interest, which means you do not pay it, but add it to the loan. In effect you are capitalising the first year's interest in advance. Doing this with an asset that increases in value means you make a large profit and reduce your tax, all with no actual cash outlay.

If this purchase was a property, the figures (very simplistically) could look as follows:

**Figure 23 Tax effect on a single property**

| | |
|---|---|
| Purchase price | 1,000,000 |
| | |
| Rent income | 45,000 |
| Expenses | |
| Depreciation | 35,000 |
| Rates and taxes | 15,000 |
| Interest on loan | 60,000 |
| Repairs | 15,000 |
| Total expenses | 125,000 |
| | |
| Net loss | –80,000 |
| Tax benefit or refund at 47% | 37,600 |
| After-tax loss | –42,400 |
| Add back depreciation (non-cash item) | 35,000 |
| Net cash loss | –7,400 |

You now have an asset worth $1 million that costs you $7400 (in the first year) to hold. As per previous chapters, if this property increases in value at 3 to 5 per cent per year the gains would be $30,000–50,000 a year, this loss will be more than offset. But now you have a starting point, something that can help you create and grow your wealth.

Taking this further, if you acquired the above property on 29 June and prepaid the first year's interest, you would receive a tax windfall of $37,600. Again, the asset must stack up, and eventually you will need to repay the loan and the interest accrued. But my point is, you are using it to purchase a great asset in a tax-effective way to yield some big upfront benefits and future gains. In some cases, this upfront benefit is the only way you can afford this first step on the property ladder.

It would not matter what the asset was, either a property or a share portfolio. The same scenario would hold true. For example, we had an engineering client with a large bill due to some one-off projects. He purchased, fully geared on 29 June, a parcel of NAB shares for around $500,000. Interest was paid in advance. This totally eliminated his tax bill. He told me later it created an interesting problem. Over the next year, the shares went up 50 per cent, which created a tax issue, but a nice one. He made $250,000, which would more than cover any tax payable thereon. The shares were hedged, so if they went down, he did not lose. It would just have cost him the interest and hedging costs (the interest was tax deductible). In an early example, I had the same tax problem, which I solved by purchasing a block of units at Campsie and prepaid one year's interest on 29 June, again eliminating a tax bill. My point is that sometimes you need to act to manage a tax problem. One way to do that is through negative gearing.

Public companies do this all the time. They acquire companies or businesses and borrow the money in order to get a massive tax write-off. The tax saved often goes a long way towards the growth of their business base and share price. Again, providing the investment is a good investment, growth is key to building wealth.

The tax refund can be a key factor in making that happen. Then, when you build the business, you avail yourself of the associated CGT and small business rollover concessions when you ultimately sell. You win both ways.

If you are a salary and wage earner with very little savings, this will be how you can obtain a big tax deduction to help offset any negative gearing losses. As mentioned earlier, sometimes the first few years can be tough. You need to recognise that negative gearing is a long-term play that will yield results in the future. In the early years, you may need to sacrifice certain things to achieve that; re-read the section on breaking the poverty trap in Chapter 3. This is vital to somehow obtaining that initial deposit to start on the property ladder. The first step will be the hardest.

## The traps and when negative gearing should not be used

Be lateral in your thinking. Use the system to leverage your investment to increase your yield and receive other benefits, like a big tax windfall or tax saving. The ultimate aim is to build wealth and a cash flow for the future, including a passive income stream. If you are subsidising your investments and you wish to give up working, then the tax benefit will no longer be relevant. Use negative gearing when your income is high and depreciation allowances will give you a massive refund. But at some stage, as your portfolio matures, you will need to start thinking differently; for example, when you move closer to retirement. It is then that you may wish to release some of the gains by selling and making your portfolio cash flow positive. It is a very difficult step and you need to be careful of tax payable on capital gains.

All businesses sometimes need a reset. They sell off assets, pay down debt and change the composition of their business. As an individual, you may also need to do the same. Focus on your best properties, reduce or reset some of your loans and increase your cash flow. Planning will be the key. For example, you may have some poor-performing properties that have some unrealised losses. It may pay to sell these, along with any properties that have a high unrealised capital gain but may have a poor rental income or perhaps a high repair bill, and retaining those that are yielding a great rental income. You may want to release some gains to pay down your mortgage on your home and then buy a new property 100 per cent geared, effectively transferring non-deductible debt for deductible debt. If you also run a business, you may be able to defer taking a wage in the year that this restructure and hence capital gain occurs. Calculate the financial and taxation effect of any restructure.

The strategy of acquiring a high number of rental properties is to create a passive income stream that replaces your 'work for a living' situation, to escape the shackles of being committed to selling your limited time for income. Negative gearing is a tool to assist part of that journey only. Later, as you move to 10 or 20 properties, you will only use it to offset the rental income and tax payable on your property portfolio. As you move to retirement or a time when you no longer work for a living, your property portfolio will slowly need to be restructured and become cash flow positive. You will now be running a business of property investment and you need to think differently.

12

# Gearing – using other people's money to create wealth

Using other people's money (OPM) is another perspective of gearing. It is not necessarily negative gearing, but gearing in its purest form; using money in the most effective way to multiply your return. It makes sense to borrow, or use other people's money, if you can earn a higher rate than the cost of that money. But be cautious of risk. In an earlier chapter, I discussed compounding and the ability to grow your assets exponentially. OPM does exactly that. By being clever, you can create extraordinary wealth by finding opportunities and selling that idea to others who can share in some of that gain. I have seen many entrepreneurs do exactly that. They make money out of an idea, and some even make extraordinary gains.

Let me focus on property, as it is a little easier to explain in numbers. However, the same holds true for loans to acquire a business or shares that you sell.

In the early 1900s, many people bought houses or other assets with cash. They did not use a bank or financial institution. However, this was a time when house prices were around a year's wages, so that was possible. Now, with house prices in Sydney being nearly ten times average earnings, this is far more difficult. Hence, you must borrow from a bank or financial institution to do so. This makes sense.

If the price of property increases over time, more than the interest you pay, then you are in front. Let's say the bank will provide a loan at 3 per cent per annum. If property prices increase by more than this amount, you are in front. Of course, you need to factor in the negative side (your holding costs) and the positive side (any rent received or, if you live in the property, the costs of your personal housing). Also factor in your ability to service any debt.

Using simple mathematics, if you have a $5 million property portfolio that is 100 per cent geared at 3 per cent, you can assume the rents or tax relief will cover the interest costs. If you hold that property portfolio for 10 years, you could expect it to be worth $10 million. You will owe the banks $5 million, which can easily be repaid by selling half of your portfolio. Hence, using other people's money has just made you $5 million. This is, of course, very simplistic. But there are many, many stories of people who have done exactly that. Timing is important, and ensuring you can service the investment is vital. Be certain that if you follow this strategy, you can weather any ups and downs, and that the income received will cover all interest costs. During the global financial crisis, many people lost everything because they could not meet their holding costs. The unfortunate part is that if they had been able to hold their investments, they would have more than doubled their gain.

Another example is using an options or extended settlement. Sometimes, a great property comes up that is underpriced. Banks often enter as mortgagee in possession and want to offload a property. Sometimes, a seller simply wants out. With a little work, you can improve its value. So, you enter into an option for, say, six months or request an extended settlement date. In the contract, you ensure that you have the right to occupy and to work on the property from the date the contract is executed. During this time, you renovate the property and have it ready for resale before settlement. You then re-advertise it at a higher price. I have seen clients do this. You have a buyer on settlement and do the purchase and sale at the same time and walk away with the profit. The only money you have put down is the deposit and renovation costs. You walk away with a healthy profit.

Many people do the same with development sites. They enter into an option at a price, arrange for a development application for a change of use to build a duplex or some other change, then sell it on at a profit before they have even purchased. Developers do this all the time.

The same holds true for business. Putting aside for a moment the business risk, if you buy a business with a bank loan at 6 per cent, and the business earns both a return for yourself and repays the loan, then you have again created wealth.

I stress, however, that there is a practical side to acquiring property or acquiring a business that is outside the scope of this book. My point is: do not be afraid of income-related debt. When used effectively, it can be a powerful wealth creation tool. Using other people's money, from a bank or a private lender, can be a powerful tool that, when handled with care, can make you extremely wealthy.

13

# Different types of investment

The strategies mentioned earlier equally apply to all asset classes. I have seen many clients follow this strategy with any or either of the classes of assets listed in Figure 24. Most eventually will have a mix of residential property, commercial property or shares in their portfolio. The reason is simple: the three classes of investments each have different types of income and a different financial strategy. The choice is never easy. It will depend on personal preferences, the skill of the investor and the strategy undertaken. I have listed each asset class with a summary of the different strategies and reasons a person may hold a certain asset. Everyone's personal situation, education and knowledge, and risk tolerance are different. Also, the younger you are, the more time you have on your side if you get it wrong. As you get older you need to take far fewer risks.

I constructed Figure 24 to simplify the various options. The choice between residential property, commercial property and shares has been a discussion raised by all investors. In most cases, it comes down to comfort, the 'sleep at night' test and personal preference. I have seen people who choose only one path and do extremely well. But like everything, it needs to be managed. With money and investment, you can never invest and forget.

**Figure 24 Classes of assets**

| | Residential property | Commercial property | Shares |
|---|---|---|---|
| Easy to understand | Yes | No | No |
| Easy to find a tenant | Yes | No | N/A |
| Possible vacancy | No | Yes | N/A |
| Marketability | 1–2 months | 6–12 months | 1 day |
| When rented, stable income | Yes | Yes | N/A |
| When vacant, a problem | No | Yes | N/A |
| Average yield | 3.50% | 7% | 0–8% |
| Income is tax paid (franked) | No | No | Yes |
| Additional tax claims like depreciation | Yes | Yes | No |
| CGT discount ownership > 12 months | Yes | Yes | Yes |
| Possible loss of capital if poorly chosen | No | No | Yes |

## Residential property

This class of asset needs little explanation. We all know from our home ownership a little about investing in rental property that will be someone's home. Rental yields will be around 3.5 per cent, which at this time covers interest costs. Depreciation allowance (for new or newer property) will tip the scale in your favour. I mentioned the Sydney prices in 1971 were $18,700 and their current price in excess of $1.5 million as a guide to possible capital gains. Generally, the only reason people will invest in residential property is the hope that they will experience the same gains. We all know that this is not always the case in the short term, but will be generally be the case in the long term. The main advantage of residential property is its marketability and ability to find another tenant with ease.

The other advantage is that, for most, it is easy to understand and control.

Given the yield is very low (unless you sell), as a rule, you need double the amount of residential property to earn the same level of income that you would from either commercial property or a fully franked share portfolio. However, some prefer it due to the inherent safety of this asset class. Also, property will take longer to sell than shares, which can be realised almost instantly, with the sale proceeds in your account within a few days.

## Commercial property

This is often overlooked by investors. Usually, they are too scared to venture into buying commercial space and then being at the mercy of a business that will be your tenant. It is true that some businesses do go broke and default on their lease. It is true that you often see vacant shops and vacant tenancies. But, while the above does happen, a vast number of businesses thrive and prosper. A vast number are extremely viable, financially solid and will be good tenants. The key is to buy quality property with a strong blue chip tenant. In most cases, you will not go wrong. The disadvantage is that businesses can experience problems. On the plus side, if you get a good property with a good tenant, you have secure long-term income. The tenant has invested heavily in your premises with improvements and overhead costs that will make them want to stay for a long time. For example, a client purchased a building that housed a Guzman y Gomez restaurant as the tenant. The restaurant invested over $400,000 in renovating the kitchen. It was not likely to move in the short term. All expenses, like rates and repairs, are paid by the tenant. Commercial property will yield around double the yield of residential property, and can be worry free. Usually, the capital gain on sale will not be as high as residential property. If you are looking for a strong rental income or return on your money, it is hard to go past commercial property.

## Share portfolios

Most people have at one time invested in shares. They have received a tip, taken the plunge and either lost or made money. However, when you look at the share market over the past 100 years, it is all up. The ASX All Ordinaries Index in 2012 was 4388, and now it is over 8400.

Figure 25 (courtesy of Wilsons Advisory) is of the ASX All Ordinaries over the past 20 years. It shows the effect of a starting point of $22,991.62 in January 2005 to an end point in January 2025 that results in $108,626.23, or an increase of 4.7 times, in the 20-year period.

**Figure 25 All Ordinaries accumulation over 20 years**

This is simply the movement in the All Ordinaries Index and not individual shares. Commonwealth Bank shares listed at $9.00 in 1991 and are now around $150.00. If you purchased 10,000 shares in 1991 for $90,000, you would have an investment worth $1.5 million today, giving you a fully franked dividend of around $4.50 per share (for 2024) or $45,000 per annum on your $90,000 investment.

We all know that choosing is everything. Investing in Microsoft, Tesla, Afterpay or many other public company floats is very much a risk. Let's look at Telstra, for example. If you chose this company while dividends have been quite low, there has not been the same capital gains. Investing in the share market is a trial-and-error path. You need to focus on spreading your investments, investing only in blue chip companies and continually monitoring the companies you invest in. Even when you do, mistakes will be made. Not every share will be a winner. You will be lucky to get it right 50 per cent of the time. In early 2025, after the Trump tariff announcement, the All Ordinaries Index dropped below 8000. It has since been on the recovery. The other important aspect with shares is that if you hold, any up and downs in the market will be unrealised gains or losses. If a share goes down (as did Commonwealth Bank shares in early 2025) you don't lose anything unless you sell.

As an accountant, I have seen the results of a lifetime of investing. I have seen many share portfolios that range from unbelievable gains to a total loss of capital. I had a client on the Central Coast that lost over $7 million (everything). I have a current client that started investing over 30 years ago with only a few hundred thousand. Every year, the cash dividends are reinvested back into more shares. Her portfolio is now over $7 million. I have seen some sharebrokers looking after client portfolios do well, while others do poorly.

Frankly, there is no certainty in share market investing. To my way of thinking, you cannot afford to have all of your eggs in one basket. The share market can be very volatile. You can only use it to have a diversity of investments and an each-way bet on investing. Having said that, if you get it right, generally the yield in the long term on share market investments will be double that of residential property and similar to commercial property. The big advantage is that dividends can be fully franked up to the current tax rate. Depending on your income and tax threshold, they will be tax paid or effectively tax free.

The share market is a vital part of your investment classes and, as you grow older, it will become more integral in providing your income stream in retirement. In your twilight years, you need to consider holding a percentage of your assets in shares due, firstly, to the franking credits and, secondly, to the easy ability to realise these assets to fund your retirement needs. This is where I suggest that your investments be managed by a professional. I wouldn't even attempt to manage this myself, as I am not close enough to the market to know what companies will prove winners. That is my view. Everyone's personal situation and risk tolerance will vary.

14

# The power of compounding – never sell

The key is in not spending time, but in investing it.

**Stephen R Covey**

Compounding is an important part of wealth creation. It uses the power of time. The question is when do you start investing and how long will it be before you retire or die? You will not know the answer to the latter, but you can guess. The point is that it is never too early or too late to start investing.

Over your lifetime, you will experience two or three property cycles. Cycles where property will have massive gains. After that, there will be a levelling off period. We have all experienced that. We have all experienced moments when we've wondered 'what if' concerning a property we sold many years ago.

We can all learn from the strategies of the richest men in the world. For example, Kerry Packer always owned all of his properties. He rarely rented any business premises. He considered rent as dead money. When he purchased Offset Alpine Printing, he entered into an option to acquire the factory at Silverwater for $700,000. Three years later, he exercised the option to acquire it. At the time, the bank valued that property at over $1.2 million. Hence, it was easy to borrow 100 per cent of the money. The point is that he purposely included the property in the deal. He never sold the property. It was a site of over one acre that took up almost an entire block in the middle of Silverwater. Offset Alpine Printing still occupies that site.

Warren Buffett has a similar strategy with his share portfolios. At the age of 52, his net wealth was US$376 million. Now 30 years later, it is a staggering US$200 billion. Warren Buffet rarely sells an asset.

The power of compounding is that you earn interest on interest, and it continues to grow because the base grows. Very few people actually sit back and look at this. They concentrate on short-term gain, 'the now'. They want instant gratification and instant gains, and so they never allow compounding to do its work. This is an important area, as it can make the difference between poverty and wealth.

By taking control of your money, you have a chance to make it grow. You must be aware of external factors like taxation, interest rate rises and inflation. I deal a lot with taxation, so it is uppermost in my mind. It is something you can often, with the right advice, limit. When you fail to adequately plan for taxation or any other major expense and so lose half of your income, the ability to compound your wealth and grow it is severely limited. No matter what you think about taxation and paying your fair share, this simple fact can make it very hard to create the financial freedom you may wish to attain.

So, what is compounding and how does it work? As a simple example, think about the median house in Sydney. In 1970, it was $18,700. Today, the figure, post-Covid-19, is edging closer to $1.5 million. In just over 50 years, the median property price has increased by an eye-watering 7921 per cent. I use this example as it is true compounding.

Compounding, by definition, is earning interest on interest. Adding the interest to the principal and earning further interest on that new principal. If you compounded monthly, the result is greater than if you compound yearly.

There are lots of ways this can be expressed. Assume the following examples:

You save, invest or deposit $100.00 per week with compounding based on monthly rests. Now remember a person works from age 18 to roughly age 65 – a total of 47 years. This will help you get this point into perspective. The compounding result is shown below:

**Figure 26 Compound interest on a weekly investment of $100 for 40 years**

| | Amount invested | Rate of return at 3% | Rate of return at 5% |
|---|---|---|---|
| 2 years or 24 months | 10,392 | 10,723 | 10,951 |
| 10 years or 120 months | 51,960 | 60,659 | 67,517 |
| 20 years | 103,920 | 142,511 | 178,719 |
| 40 years | 207,840 | 401,986 | 663,520 |

The example is just $100.00 per week. It is not even inflation adjusted. Imagine if you adjusted for inflation the $100.00 per week. The result is over $1 million dollars. This is a savings plan that you could easily set up as an automated payment from your salary into a separate saving/investment account. You could also salary sacrifice this amount into your super (more on that later). You would never miss it. The effect is an unbelievable additional $663,520 in retirement savings.

**Figure 27 Compounding one cent and doubling it every day**

| Day | Amount | Total |
|---|---:|---:|
| 1 | $ 0.01 | $ 0.01 |
| 2 | $ 0.02 | $ 0.03 |
| 3 | $ 0.04 | $ 0.07 |
| 4 | $ 0.08 | $ 0.15 |
| 5 | $ 0.16 | $ 0.31 |
| 6 | $ 0.32 | $ 0.63 |
| 7 | $ 0.64 | $ 1.27 |
| 8 | $ 1.28 | $ 2.55 |
| 9 | $ 2.56 | $ 5.11 |
| 10 | $ 5.12 | $ 10.23 |
| 11 | $ 10.24 | $ 20.47 |
| 12 | $ 20.48 | $ 40.95 |
| 13 | $ 40.96 | $ 81.91 |
| 14 | $ 81.92 | $ 163.83 |
| 15 | $ 163.84 | $ 327.67 |
| 16 | $ 327.68 | $ 655.35 |
| 17 | $ 655.36 | $ 1,310.71 |
| 18 | $ 1,310.72 | $ 2,621.43 |
| 19 | $ 2,621.44 | $ 5,242.87 |
| 20 | $ 5,242.88 | $ 10,485.75 |
| 21 | $ 10,485.76 | $ 20,971.51 |
| 22 | $ 20,971.52 | $ 41,943.03 |
| 23 | $ 41,943.04 | $ 83,886.07 |
| 24 | $ 83,886.08 | $ 167,772.15 |
| 25 | $ 167,772.16 | $ 335,544.31 |
| 26 | $ 335,544.32 | $ 671,088.63 |
| 27 | $ 671,088.64 | $ 1,342,177.27 |
| 28 | $ 1,342,177.28 | $ 2,684,354.55 |
| 29 | $ 2,684,354.56 | $ 5,368,709.11 |
| 30 | $ 5,368,709.12 | $ 10,737,418.23 |
| 31 | $ 10,737,418.24 | $ 21,474,836.47 |

Let me explain another example to illustrate my point (this is an old joke, but a good one). You apply for a job. The employer offers you either $1 million if you work for them for 30 days or to give you a cent a day and double it every day for 30 days. What would you choose? Which pay option will give you the highest income? If you take the $1 million, that is all you will get. But let's consider the 'cent a day' option. One cent becomes two; two become four; four become eight; eight becomes 16. After eight days, it is $2.55. After 15 days, you will have received only $327.67. You are starting to think that with half the month gone, the $1 million upfront would have been the best option. It is slow initially, but it really builds up. It gives you exponential growth. This is what happens with compounding. After 30 days, your total income is $10,737,418.23, or at 31 days, it is $21,474,838.47.

Look at Figure 27. This is the true power of compounding. It is almost unbelievable, but as an accountant, I can tell you that the figures do not lie.

Let's look at this with an interest factor of, say, 5 per cent and bring to account the effect taxation will have on your rate of return.

From your school days, you will probably remember the following formula for compound interest:

$$A = P(1 + \frac{r}{n})^{nt}$$

Where:

A = the amount you will end up with

P = the original principal amount

R = rate of interest as a decimal

N = number of periods (12 for 12 months or 52 for 52 weeks)

T = time in periods (months or years)

For example, you have $1000 earning 5 per cent, compounding monthly for 15 years. This becomes:

A = $1000(1+(0.05/12))×(12×15)

A = $1000 ((1.00417)×(180))

A = $2113.70

Hence, it has doubled in 15 years, earning a mere 5 per cent rate of return. Imagine if, along the way, there were a few years where the interest was, say, 10 per cent. This could reduce the doubling time to only 10 years. Imagine if, at the end of each year, you lose 30 per cent of the income in taxation. This will extend the doubling period to more than 20 years.

This is why, at a personal level, superannuation, property and other long-term assets, if retained long enough, can give you the above eye-watering gains.

Now you understand the power of compounding, you need to use it to accumulate wealth. This simple factor was probably never taught to you at school or even university. Your parents probably never discussed it. If you are a parent reading this book, please discuss this with your children as, for them, the difference can be life-changing. I know they will want to use their pocket money for the latest iPhone, that saving for retirement or a university degree of some future purpose will be hard to swallow. But maybe take them for a visit to the Salvation Army or Red Cross. Go down any main street of any capital city and you will see the homeless. Show them what happens to people who do not have sufficient money to own a house, provide for their own living or support themselves. As I have said many times, the government cannot be relied upon to meet the basic needs of retirees in the future. Ask any pensioner how tough it is to survive on a pension even now, knowing that the purchasing power of the current pension is about to get reduced because of inflation. In the past 20 years, pensions have never kept up with increases in the cost of living. This problem is about to get worse.

Albert Einstein described compounding as 'the eighth wonder of the world'. He said, 'He who understands it, earns it. He who doesn't, pays it.'

George S Clason, in his book, *The Richest Man in Babylon*, covered the power of compounding and saving small amounts that accumulate into large sums with compounding. It was first published in 1926 and continues to be a bestseller. It is about how small savings accumulate wealth over time. It is as true today as it was in 1926. I recommend that everyone read this book.

15

# What investment strategy should I follow?

## Your home must be paid off

You must pay your home off. This must be the first investment you make. This will set you up for the future. I have already covered the tax aspects, so very little more needs to be said. However, I want to make a very strong point here. Firstly, do not fall for the high-debt McMansion scenario. Buy what you can afford. Buy in a suburb that may not be the best suburb but should in time improve. Buy close to a capital city, usually no more than about 15 kilometres out. Somewhere close to schools and public transport. My first home was in Wiley Park in Western Sydney, a unit near the train station in an old blonde brick building, not flash but affordable. At 21 years old, I could not afford anything better. This unit cost $21,500 and I borrowed $18,500 (it is probably worth in excess of $500,000 today). Now here's the thing. As soon as you purchase, you should immediately make additional payments. Compounding, as discussed earlier, on a home loan works in the bank's favour, not yours. A few extra dollars per week can cut years off your loan. Try to do this as early as you can on the loan. Don't get complacent and simply agree to the 30-year mortgage. What you are trying to do is reduce the non-tax deductible interest for future investment purposes. So work like crazy to pay off, reduce or eliminate your first home loan. Drive an old car, reduce your spending on clothes, entertaining and anything not aligned to your goal to retire wealthy. Compounding is what you are trying to do here. By putting small amounts into your mortgage, you will compound the effect and eventually be debt free. The goal should always be to have your sole and principal residence debt free. You may use it as security later, but only for investment purposes that will yield a return for which any loans will be tax deductible.

## Rental property

You need more than your sole and principal residence to create a future nest egg that will give you enough passive income to achieve the freedom to quit your day job, if you want to. Rental properties can be either residential or commercial, or a mixture of both. Now here is the key. You must buy the right properties. Buy with your brain, not your heart. Buy only what will stack up. Be careful of off-the-plan purchases. Remember the Lindy effect: the longer something has been around, the longer it's likely to persist into the future. It's based on the idea that things that have stood the test of time are things that you can rely on. Warren Buffett and Kerry Packer were big proponents of this adage. James Packer, when he strayed into an investment in One.Tel, lost $376 million. Kerry was furious at the time.

The next step is to hold that asset. Set the strategy and hold the course. It is hard to be exact on how many properties you need, as it would depend on their value, but I would guess somewhere in excess of five with no debt. This strategy is outlined further in the book, in far more detail. Use the power of compounding to build a massive portfolio that will yield a passive income that will give you choices in life.

## Shares

Choosing a share investment is the job of professional stockbrokers, but they do not always get it right. The reason is simple: there are so many external factors that can influence the success of any particular company. If the professionals cannot get it right, what chance does the average person have, who does not have the benefit or access to research that professionals have? As far as I am concerned, any person, unless they have some insider knowledge (which is illegal by the way), has very little chance in selecting short-term wins and losses on the stock market.

But again, the Lindy effect (as mentioned earlier) helps with long-term gains. Over time, the share market as a whole will grow and outpace inflation and any other indicator. Look again at Figure 25, on page 94.

A simple example is two household names. Commonwealth Bank shares, when listed in 1991, were $9.00 per share. These shares today are worth around $150.00, a gain of over 1500 per cent. Telstra, on the other hand, listed at $3.30 in 1999. The current price is $3.85. You can see how hard it is to get it right.

I know you are thinking I am too small an investor to consider the share market. But that is not true. In fact, your superannuation is more than likely invested into the share market. There are also a number of small share-trading apps that allow you to purchase the index. However, be aware that, whether you invest via indexes or on the market as a whole, buying shares is a holding game. It is not a 'get rich quick' scheme. If you are nervous and want to do daily checks on how your investments are going, then this is probably not the investment you should choose.

Often, accountants are asked to give financial advice. However, accountants are not licensed to do so unless they do extra study and become a licensed financial planner. This is a road I went down in 2018. In looking at this area, I came across a study of human behaviours as it related to share investing. It is called the DALBAR study. It looked at the emotional side of investing and why most people sell at the wrong time and buy at the wrong time. It helped me understand why my share investing didn't work. It is a very interesting correlation between emotion and buying/selling habits, a risk profile that investors need to be aware of. The DALBAR's Quantitative Analysis of Investor Behavior (QAIB) measures the effects of investor decisions to buy, sell and switch into and out of mutual funds over short- and long-term timeframes. The results consistently show that the average investor earns less – in many cases, much less – than mutual fund performance reports would suggest. Having worked with Kerry Packer, he seemed to have an intuition about this. He always seemed to know when to hold and when to fold (as the Kenny Rogers song 'The Gambler' goes). However, the DALBAR studies prove that the average investor generally gets this wrong. They get emotional when they see their investment starting to deteriorate. They panic and sell, thus realising the capital losses. Then when the market starts to rise, they come back too late and miss most of the gains. If they did nothing, usually with blue chip shares, they will recover.

Warren Buffett's philosophy is to only buy well-known blue chip shares. He also has a 'hold forever' type strategy. Invest only in the top 100 blue chip shares and then simply stay in the market. Set and forget. Easier said than done. Be like my client, Mrs G, who has 20 top stocks with a value now of over $7 million (cost less than $2m), but in fact her initial investments were, over time, only a few hundred thousand. The rest is dividend reinvestments – 30 years' worth ... and earning a dividend of nearly $300,000 per annum. Unless you have specific knowledge in the share market, don't be a share trader; be a share investor for the long term.

## Superannuation

This is a must-have additional part of your investment strategy for two important reasons:

1. It is extremely tax advantageous. In accumulation mode (before you retire), income earned by the fund and your tax deductible contributions are taxed at only 15 per cent (subject to certain caps).
2. At retirement phase (when you retire or meet a condition of release), it is a tax-free vehicle – up to the balance transfer caps of $1.9 million per member. The income on this extra balance is taxed at 15 per cent.

You will already have a balance in your super fund if you are working. Your employer is obligated to pay 11.5 per cent (rising to 12% on 1 July 2025) of your salary to a complying superannuation fund (or your self-managed super fund). So never forget this balance and work with it. It may not be your 'early in life' investment strategy, but it will become very important later in life as you reach retirement age or as a condition of release (which may only be 60 years old).

I have always seen super as an each-way bet; in other words, a really safe nest egg that is a 'set and forget' investment that, with the passage of time and the power of compounding, will grow into something of value. If you are in business or if you are taking risks on various investment strategies, your superannuation nest egg should not be caught up in the strategies. This must be a safe harbour, in case you get other areas of your investments wrong. We all know that this can happen, so don't be tempted to make early release withdrawals or to roll the balance into a self-managed super fund and then increase your risks by trying to do better than your industry fund. Think of this nest egg as a fallback position. As you come closer to retirement, you should start increasing your superannuation balances. As stated earlier, superannuation is a tax-advantaged environment. The key will be how to transition some of your investments into this tax-advantaged environment.

For example, I was playing golf one Sunday morning. I had got to know the course marshal really well. It is amazing what people tell me when they know I am an accountant. He was talking (well, complaining) about his tax. He said that he sold his house and put the money in the bank. He was complaining about the extra tax he was paying on the interest he was earning. He was 70 years old and looking to retire shortly. The tax solution was so easy that I cannot understand why he didn't think of it. He simply needed to put the proceeds of the house sale into his super fund. He would need to use either the downsizer rule ($300,000 per member) and/or three-year carried forward rule (3 × $120,000 per member), depending on the amount, to allow the lump sum transfer. Then make sure the fund was in pension mode. If he needed money to live on, he could make unlimited tax-free withdrawals from his fund. His tax would have been zero on all of the above, a simple strategy that could save him many thousands of dollars.

16

# What not to do – clients that have got it wrong

In 1930 in one of his famous talks, Earl Nightingale discussed why most people do not save sufficient money for their future (retirement) needs. It was as true then as it is today. In Australia, it is a sad fact that 95 per cent of the population will retire broke. By broke, I mean without sufficient income to live on without some form of financial assistance or support. This support usually comes from either family or government.

Some consider it a rite of passage when they get older to be able to still qualify for an aged pension. Believe it or not, I have seen people go on massive overseas trips to spend their money, just to qualify for the pension. Well, wake up, Australia! The cost of pensions to the government, as our population ages, will be such a drain on the economy that the government will be forced to reduce the pension. If it is not reduced, it will simply not be increased in line with CPI, which will have the same effect over time: reducing it to below the poverty line.

When the aged pension was introduced in 1909, less than 5 per cent of the population lived beyond 65 years old. Today, the reverse is true. How the government will fund a future pension that enables a person sufficient income to survive is very unclear. Given the pressure on the public purse due to support packages, such as those provided during the Covid-19 pandemic, it is highly likely that the government will be unable to sustain anywhere near the current levels of social welfare. The solution is to look after yourself and to not rely on a government hand-out that will simply not be there.

Why do many people get their investment strategies wrong? What do they do that is wrong, and how can you avoid the trap of following the masses off the cliff into financial oblivion or worse?

Investor behaviour is not simply buying and selling at the wrong time. There are psychological traps, triggers and misconceptions that can cause an investor to act irrationally. This irrationality leads to buying and selling at the wrong time, which in turn will lead to poor performance loss and a 'it's not for me' attitude. After all, we are all human. As I mentioned earlier, luck can also play a part. If you time a market wrong, through no fault of yours, that feeling of failure can put you off in the future. These factors are defined in the following list, not that this would make you feel better if a pandemic just wiped out 30 per cent of your share portfolio:

1. Loss aversion – expecting to find high returns with low risk.
2. Narrow framing – making decisions without considering all implications.
3. Mental accounting – taking undue risk in one area and avoiding rational risk in another.
4. Diversification – seeking to reduce risk, but simply using different sources of the same thing.
5. Anchoring – relating to the familiar experiences, even when inappropriate.

6. Herding – copying the behaviours of others, even in the face of unfavourable outcomes.
7. Regret – treating errors of commission paid to advisors more seriously than errors of omission. In other words focusing on the short-term costs (commission) rather than the long-term strategy. It also includes buyer's remorse, which can sometimes be unfounded and the result of overthinking the decision.
8. Media response – tendency to react to news without reasonable explanation.
9. Optimism – belief that good things happen to me and bad things happen to others.
10. On the reverse side, the fear of missing out often causes irrational and unresearched decision making.

Whenever I have tried to guess the market, I have got it wrong. With share investments, you need to set and forget. Also remember the aspect of dollar cost averaging. By entering the market in small ways, whether it is at a high or a low, you are using the power of time to smooth out any ups and downs.

## Better to have loved and lost than to never have loved at all

My message is simple. In business and in life you need to have a go. Sometimes you get it wrong. Sometimes small factors work against you. Sometimes it is simply bad luck. Timing and external factors are matters outside your control that can cause loss. Brad Pitt drops in and your wife is besotted with him and runs away. His good looks and millions in the bank are too hard for her to refuse. Is it your fault? Of course not! Can you recover? Most definitely yes. Can you learn from it? Again, definitely yes.

My example might be far-fetched, but I want to impress on you that things can happen that may not be in your control. Coming back from it makes you better and stronger. In your journey to financial freedom, there will always be bumps along the way. What sets you apart is being able to ride out these bumps and keep moving forward in a straight line.

The Covid-19 pandemic is a prime example. Life suddenly took on a different meaning. How did you handle Covid-19? Did you sit in a corner and cry? Did you think, 'Wow, this is a total re-alignment of my thinking'? Did you know that, while some people suffered and needed to use the early super release scheme to access money for rent and other necessities, others made more money than ever before?

Let me recount three examples.

One client in the entertainment industry had no work. They sat at home in self-pity and drew $10,000 from their super just for living costs. But I noticed on Facebook that the husband purchased an anniversary diamond ring to celebrate their many years of marriage and devotion to each other, which must have cost around $5000.

Another client sold women's clothing through shops and online. When Covid-19 hit, all the shop sales dropped dramatically. My client immediately improved their website, spent money on upgrading the shopping cart, increasing clothing lines and added new photographs. They had Zoom meetings with suppliers and designers. As a result, through the Covid-19 pandemic, they made more than $1 million in profit. Life-changing, in a positive way.

I am the third example. I owned my office building and had around eight staff. I had purchased the building based on the growth I knew would happen. Hence, I could accommodate a team of about 12. The day after the Prime Minister announced the restrictions, I went into an empty office. It was so soul-destroying. Our business dropped by over 70 per cent and our staff stayed home. Wages and overheads still needed to be paid. Would anyone bother about their tax return lodgements when there was a fear of dying from Covid-19? You can imagine why accounting and tax took a back seat. However, I wasn't about to let that defeat me. The government issued all sorts of relief measures, some very complicated and some hard to access. I set about reading, understanding and putting together a booklet on all of the measures available, both at a federal level and a state level. I distributed it free on Facebook through a number of business groups I was in. We had lots of calls for help, some of which I did free of charge. It took some time, but about three months after the initial shock of Covid-19 subsided, things started to pick up. The result was that the business grew about 30 per cent and built a reputation as a go-to firm for advice.

In retrospect, think about the poor decisions you have made and think about what you could have done better. If you purchased an overpriced property by listening to the spruiking of an agent and it will take time to recover the costs, then make a business decision on what to do. Don't throw in the towel and give up. Every life story you read will give you examples of when a mistake has been made. It is how you deal with that going forward that will be the deciding factor on whether you will be able to create a level of wealth that will support the lifestyle you seek. As the saying goes, when the world throws you lemons, don't quit and say 'poor me'; make lemon juice and sell it. If you are new to investments, try to not be ruled by emotion. Review the ten points listed in this chapter. Try to act from a place of research and knowledge.

Part 3

# Case studies of what others have done

No one shoe fits all. I have met many self-made millionaires who had made their money in ways that they were comfortable doing. That may have been by creating a business, buying shares over a 30-year period, working two jobs to buy their first house or simply working for a company for 30 years to eventually rise to be a director on a massive salary with share options.

Trust me when I say the majority of wealth in Australia is made through property ownership. The above are exceptions.

The purpose of this section is to simply explain actual case studies of what others have done, including myself, to create wealth and passive income that allows me to never work again, should I so choose. Remember, this an important decision that needs to be in your hands. It gives you freedom, and the people I see in this situation have a smile on their faces. But just because you may never need to work again doesn't mean you don't need purpose in life. Generally, most people who are wealthy never quit and lose that purpose. But they are free to choose. They take nice holidays, help their family and generally lead a fulfilling life.

Broadly these case studies are actual situations where clients (or I) have used one or more of the following four ways to be wealthy:

1. Principal place of residence – trading, improving, redeveloping, subdividing, and so on.
2. Owning a number of residential properties that are rented.
3. Purchasing commercial properties.
4. Building a large share portfolio.

17

# Principal place of residence (PPR)

I know I have discussed this many times in this book, but I want to get the message across that this is a massive tax haven for investment. I have made many millions of dollars, tax free, by buying well, improving and then selling. While I have also been able to do other things tax free, it is harder and requires a lot of structuring that is sometimes not possible to do.

Let me be clear on this: if you enter into a purchase for the sole and dominant reason to make money, then under the tax act, any gains will be taxable. If, however, you acquire an asset for some other purpose, say a place to live, and then do things to make a realisation of the property more saleable in a viable manner to, say, increase the realisation price, then that is an ancillary reason and not the sole and dominant purpose for the acquisition. I am sure you can read between the lines on this. This point is explained in more detail in the tax section at Chapter 22 regarding intent and purpose. Do not allow yourself to be trapped by the tax office by getting the *intent* wrong.

There are two ways to make tax-free gains on your PPR. The first is to buy, hold, renovate and then sell. I did this with a property

I owned at Bayview on the Northern Beaches. I paid $680,000 for a house on the hill, renovated it over a ten-year period, spent about $300,000 and sold it for $1.8 million.

The other way is to subdivide. My aunt purchased a property a Woolooware (near Cronulla). It was a large block. She paid around $500,000 for it, then subdivided the rear block and sold it for $650,000. She renovated the front house and sold it for $950,000. What a great investment. Now this will not be totally tax free. The rear block will be subject to some tax, as a new asset has been created. I will explain in more detail the tax consequences of this and how to minimise it. Also, it does take time to get council approvals for this. Again, be cautious of the intent and manner in which the above is carried out. It must be ancillary to the main aim and a simple realisation of a capital asset in the most effective way. This is covered in more detail in the tax section of this book.

I am in the process of doing the same thing at my home. I acquired it almost ten years ago. The property is heritage listed and on three titles. It has taken nearly eight years to get council approval. This didn't matter as it was our home and we were in no hurry to do the development. On an adjoining lot, we are building two houses. Construction has finally commenced. The original house and the two additional houses will make a total of three homes on the original site. Now comes the complicated part: what will be subject to capital gains tax and what will be tax free? Our plan is to sell the original house and move into one of the new houses. The sale of the original house will be tax free and the house we move into will be tax free, should we ever sell it. The third house, after deducting a portion of the original land costs plus the build costs, will be taxable when and if sold. If I hold it for 12 months and rent it out, only 50 per cent of the gain will be taxable.

I have done some extensive tax modelling on this to calculate exactly the taxable components. I don't want to give too much away, but this investment has resulted in the biggest gain I have ever made. Some would say that you cannot live on gains built up in the value of your home. But those that say that do not see the bigger picture. As you move closer to retirement, your children will leave home and you will more than likely start to think about downsizing. Hence, you can release the stored value in your home to help fund your retirement. While I always consider that you need many strings to your wealth bow, your home can be an important and integral part. The strange part is that anyone can do this. Investments with this sort of potential appear all the time. You just need to have an open mind. I have seen many clients do similar things. I know there is a risk, but faint heart never won fair maiden.

Your PPR should be an important, if not vital, part of your investment strategy.

## 18

# Residential rental property portfolio – using the tax system

A relative and her husband were complaining about not getting anywhere financially. I am sure you, as the reader, can relate to that. They were both on high incomes, working for either government bodies or similar, paying lots of tax, with very little to show for it.

I remember the incident extremely well. We were sitting on my verandah in Bayview, Sydney, having a few drinks and they started to open up. My answer was very simple – and actually forms the basis of the strategies in this book.

I asked how risk-adverse they were. Would they sleep at night if they borrowed heavily to buy assets and needed to wait for them to increase? If they purchased assets and, for a short time those assets dropped or did not go up in value, would they be okay with that and not panic? The answer was they were okay with risk and were happy to take a long-term view.

Of course, I wasn't recommending a winner for the Melbourne Cup or a share investment that would be the next Microsoft, but something far plainer and less intriguing.

I explained they should consider buying rental property with 100 per cent gearing. They should do this every year or as the market dictated. They should do their own homework and not rely on a real estate agent's market assessment. They shouldn't be too concerned about small overpayments if the market was okay, the tenant was good and the property had good long-term benefits.

First, they completed renovating their home. That gave them the equity to borrow. They then purchased their first investment house. They were a little concerned about risk, so they purchased it in partnership with other family members. Following is a listing of the properties they purchased. The figures and years are approximated, as I wasn't privy to every purchase:

- House 1 – $350,000 in Gosford; now worth $1.2 million.
- House 2 – $550,000 in Point Frederick renovated and subdivided. Sold for $1.5 million.
- House 3 – $850,000 in Wamberal; now worth $1.5 million.
- Unit 1 – $350,000 in Erina; now worth $400,000.
- Commercial property 1 – $650,000 in Taree; now worth $1.4 million.
- Townhouse 1 – $250,000 in Gosford; now worth $350,000.
- They then purchased another five properties.
- Their total portfolio is approximately $9 million.

For the first few years, the interest cost and depreciation exceeded the rent. They received massive tax refunds. They continued to buy and, in the next ten years, acquired in excess of ten properties, most of which they still own. Yes, they made a few mistakes and got a few wrong. Some property repairs were a bit excessive; some tenants were problem tenants and needed managing. But on the whole, over the ten- to 15-year period, they have been able to accumulate wealth, such that they have now retired from work and have a net worth (I am guessing) of more than $10 million, with great rental income. They no longer need to work. True story.

The tax benefits can make building up a property portfolio possible. The benefits of owning rental properties are fourfold. It is why property is the preferred option for wealth creation over other types of investments.

First, any losses resulting from holding the properties (where rents do not cover other costs) are offset to other income and result in tax refunds (or you could say an ATO tax subsidy). Losses incurred in operating a business as a sole trader are generally (subject to some rules) not able to be offset to salary income and are quarantined to be offset against future business income. This is due to the non-commercial loss provisions, which list out a number of conditions that must be satisfied to offset these losses to your salaried and wage income.

Second, non-cash items like depreciation are deductible and add to the tax loss and, hence, to refunds.

Third, providing the property is retained for at least 12 months, only 50 per cent of any net gain will be taxable.

Fourth, you only pay tax on realised gains. You do not pay tax on any increase in value until you sell.

19

# Commercial property portfolio

The following is a real situation that occurred about four years ago. I have a client in the motor vehicle bodywork repair business. The previous five years, the business had been great. My client had paid off their home and had surplus money in the bank. Let's call them Bill and Sue. I had finished their year-end work and was sitting in their lounge room talking. Bill said to me that he was worried. While they had some money aside, he felt that if his business deteriorated for any reason, or he could not work as hard as he had been, they would not be able to live the life they were currently living (or his wife was accustomed to living). He also complained that, on the money he had saved, he was earning less than 1 per cent. But he didn't know what to do.

We talked for a while about residential investments, shares or buying another business and various other investments. But nothing suited. Frankly, he wasn't comfortable as, for him, the risks were too high. Residential investments provide capital gains in time, but Bill felt he didn't want to wait. He didn't want to buy blue chip shares or engage an investment broker as he felt he would lose control.

The decision was made to look at creating a commercial property portfolio. I suggested we aim to create a $10 million portfolio of commercial properties with only blue chip tenants; nothing risky or requiring work. We set up a property trust to be the investment vehicle (unit trust). The first property that became available to look at was a building that housed a Guzman y Gomez (GYG) company-owned restaurant. We reviewed all the numbers, inspected it, made offers, all the normal parts of the buying process. We approached the bank to borrow just over 50 per cent of the purchase price. The investment stacked up and an offer was made and accepted. He paid $2.4 million for the building, with a rent yield of 6 per cent. This proved to be the base for the next four years. GYG paid all outgoings. The agent managed it. It was a truly 'set and forget' investment. GYG even renewed the lease for a further five plus five years with a small rental increase.

Over the next four years, Bill and Sue acquired another four properties. Last year, the investment trust made a profit of $600,000. It has properties worth around $11 million, with amounts owing to the bank of $7 million. In other words, they have unrealised gains of over $4 million. Not bad for four years and an initial $1.2 million deposit.

Bill and Sue are very savvy investors. They really looked hard at every investment acquisition and spent time making sure they were comfortable with the property and the tenant. They also keep a close eye on the tenants and the rents.

At first, they were very apprehensive on this path. They did not fully understand commercial properties and were worried about the risks. But with an anchor tenant like Guzman y Gomez, these risks were mitigated. Generally, with commercial properties, the tenant pays all outgoings, including repairs, council rates, water rates and land tax, if applicable. In four years, Bill and Sue's initial investment of $1.2 million now yields an annual net return of $600,000 per annum and has a capital growth of $4 million. Imagine what the next ten years will look like. Again, a true story.

## Part 4

# What structure do you hold your investments in?

Deciding what structure to hold your investments in is a very important factor. The considerations will be the following:

1. Tax planning – can I offset initial losses against my other income (for example, my salary)?
2. Do I need to protect my assets if I am sued? Am I in a profession or business that carries litigation risk, like a doctor? Perhaps you have been married a few times and need to protect your assets against future spouses for the benefit of your children in an earlier marriage or just your own retirement needs.
3. Do I want to quarantine my investment portfolio for future generations, such as providing assistance to my children and future grandchildren?

This is not to mention the myriad tax consequences that may follow that are needed to build wealth.

My experience is that in the early stages of wealth creation, the structure you use may need changing as your circumstances change. Usually, the first few investments, if they are massively negatively geared, may need to be purchased in your personal name, if you're on a high income. Then, as time goes by and the investments become positively geared, they need to be held in a different structure. They may even need to be sold for tax reasons.

The other important consideration is land tax. This is a state government tax that is levied on landholders. Assets held in trusts pay a higher land tax amount than if held personally. However, each state has various tax-free thresholds that will limit the tax payable. Working out which type of entity in which to hold assets is complicated and not an exact science. To get it right needs careful planning, a crystal ball and the skills of prediction. Who ever said that tax planning was easy?

20

# Tax structures to hold assets

The question of what type of entity you use to acquire an asset needs to be answered every time you purchase a property. This is because what may have applied in earlier years or with other asset purchases may not be relevant with the asset you are now wishing to purchase. Unfortunately, it is also the case that what may be the right structure when you start this journey may not be the right structure for future acquisitions.

Just to recap, every type of structure has different tax and legal consequences. With property in particular, there are three things to consider:

1. If you intend on living in the property, to get the principal place of residence (PPR) exemption, it must be in your personal name. This also applies to land tax exemptions. A property is exempt from land tax if it is your PPR. If the property is held in a trust, in some states you can also obtain a PPR exemption. But be aware you can only have one PPR. A holiday home or second property cannot also be your PPR, even if it is not rented and only used by you.

2. If the property is an investment property and the property has tax losses, you cannot offset these tax losses against your other income unless the property ownership and your income are aligned. For example, if the property is owned by yourself and your spouse, and one has high income and the other has no income, the losses must be applied in accordance with the ownership structure of the property. If the property is held by yourself and your partner as joint tenants, then from a tax point of view it will be treated at 50 per cent each. Losses will be applied based on this. If it is as tenants in common and the percentages are defined, the tax deductions will be based on these ownership percentages. They cannot be changed without incurring transfer duty.
3. If you are in a litigious profession or work environment, such as a doctor, you may wish to think about asset protection. This also applies to family separation and estate planning. If the property is in your personal name, it will be caught as part of your assets and available to creditors. This will also apply if you are in a de facto relationship and seek to shelter your assets from any family law court claim (which incidentally is almost impossible to do).

So, before you decide which entity to use, think about whether any of these three situations apply to you. This will ensure that there are no unintended future consequences.

Let's review the various structures that are available to use to purchase a property. As a PPR would generally be in your own personal name (or names), the following would generally apply to the purchase of investment properties. This list is a very simplistic outline of the types of structures and some key points as they relate to property purchases:

- **Buying in your own personal name.** While from an asset protection point of view this may be dangerous, it is generally preferred for property purchases that may lose money and hence be negatively geared. The loans and therefore all liabilities will be in your name as the registered owner. Any profits or losses will become your profit or loss. Any capital gains will become your capital gain and taxed at your marginal tax rate. If it is an investment property, you will be able to avail yourself of the 50 per cent capital gains discount on any capital gain. Capital losses cannot be offset to other income (like your salary), but can be carried forward indefinitely to be offset against any future capital gains.
- **As joint owners with your spouse, a family member or a company or trust.** In other words, as a partnership. The net income (profit or loss) will be shared by the partners. Also, all partners will be jointly and severely liable for all debts of the partnership. This will not be in proportion to their partnership interest, but each and every partner will be equally liable for all debts. Profits are distributed to the partners in accordance with the partnership agreement. If no agreement exists, then it will be distributed equally. This income will be added to any other income they have earned and will be taxed at each partner's marginal rate

of tax. If partners are added or leave, the old partnership ceases and a new partnership is created, which will have capital gains tax implications (deemed sale). Losses in a partnership are distributed to the partners in the same manner as income. This is not the case with trusts. In a trust, losses are locked up in the trust.

- **Using a company, meaning a proprietary limited (Pty Ltd) company (not a business name).** A company is registered with the Australian Securities and Investment Commission (ASIC) as having a share capital, directors and a constitution confirming the rules that apply to its operations. The company is liable (not the directors or shareholders) for all debts, except where certain laws can pierce this corporate veil and attack the directors personally. Tax is levied at either 25 per cent or 30 per cent, depending on whether the company is a base rate entity or earns passive income. If the company's main trading is to own property and receive passive income, it is taxed at 30 per cent on its net profit. New shareholders can come and go without affecting the business, but may trigger some carried forward loss provisions and, in some states, may trigger stamp duty on the share transfer at similar rates to stamp duty on property purchases. Each state has a different tax-free threshold on such share transfers, which in effect enables the property to be transferred by transferring the ownership of the shares held in the company. The biggest disadvantage for a company is the inability to claim the 50 per cent CGT discount. A company will pay tax on the full gain made and can pass on to shareholders this gain as a franked dividend, in effect passing on the tax credit to the shareholder. However, it still will not negate the fact that tax is payable on the entire capital gain rather than only 50 per cent of the gain. For this reason, owning property in a company is not the preferred option.

- **In a discretionary trust or family trust (usually the same).** A trust is an arrangement established via a trust deed that sets out how the asset will be managed. It must have a trustee and beneficiaries. The trustee runs the trust and makes all the decisions on how it is to operate. Generally, this will be a company (corporate trustee) for liability reasons. All profits must be distributed to beneficiaries (usually individuals or person) to avoid a higher tax being levied on the trustee. Liabilities sit with the trustee, who will indemnify itself against the trust assets. Tax is at the beneficiary level, which is usually family members. Losses are trapped in a trust and cannot be passed on to beneficiaries (which they can in a partnership). Gains, which include capital gains, are distributed to the beneficiaries as decided by the trustee, hence the term discretionary trust. While a capital gain will also be distributed to the beneficiaries, the 50 per cent CGT discount on any capital gain is also available to be offset by the beneficiaries against this gain. To complicate matters, beneficiaries can also be companies or other entities.
- **In a unit or property trust.** This is very similar to the discretionary trust, but instead of having a discretionary

option with respect to profits, the unit trust must declare profits in accordance with the units issued by the trust to the unit holders (similar to shareholders). Losses also are trapped in a unit trust and cannot be passed on to unit holders. A property trust will have slightly different rules regarding profit distributions and is used to retain the land tax thresholds in the entity. In most states, a property trust must have within its trust deed a clause prohibiting foreign persons or foreign entities owning units in the trust. Otherwise, higher land tax will be payable. A property trust is an ideal vehicle to create a separate property portfolio, especially a commercial property portfolio.

- **Using a superannuation fund (meaning usually a self-managed superannuation fund).** A superannuation fund can own property and can, with the use of a limited recourse borrowing arrangement (LRBA), borrow money to acquire a property. But this is very limited and very restrictive. The main reason you would buy a property in your super fund would be to use the cash balance in your super fund as the deposit. For example, you may have a balance in an industry fund that you wish to rollover into a self-managed fund to acquire a property. As a word of warning, this would be putting your entire superannuation nest egg in one asset and, unless you have a mix of assets outside of super, it would generally not be a good idea. However, the benefits are twofold. First, a super fund in accumulation mode pays tax at 15 per cent on its earnings. In pension mode, it is tax free. Hence, any capital gains during pension mode will be tax free. When the fund is in accumulation mode, capital gains are taxed at 10 per cent. Personally, I feel when your portfolio outside of super gets high, you may consider purchasing a property in super that will yield a great return both from an income and capital gains point of view.

- **Other structures** include public companies, public trading trusts, not-for-profit entities and various other charitable trusts. These are outside the scope of this book.

From my point of view, you would more than likely hold various properties in various structures. For example, you may hold some very highly leveraged property in your own name to offset the tax payable on your income. You may hold some commercial property in a unit trust or discretionary trust to shield the land tax thresholds or to enable the net income to be distributed in a tax-effective way. You may also hold a property in your super fund that has no debt and so is positively geared. You would hold this property in your super fund until you reach retirement age (or reach a condition of release), when the fund would be in pension mode and totally tax free. For example, if a property was purchased ten years before retirement and was held continuously in your fund, any accrued gains will be free from any capital gains tax the moment the fund (or members) move to pension mode.

It is also the case that you may wish to acquire each property in a different trust. For example, a bank will sometimes be very restrictive on their lending and want to take a charge or guarantee over the entity holding the asset. If this entity owns a few properties, this will be a problem for the other lenders. Hence, if you are using different banks for loans, you may wish to consider creating different entities for each property purchase. This would also be the case where you have different investors or family members involved. It will help keep the structures separate.

21

# Tax payable using different ownership structures

In the midst of chaos, there is also opportunity.

**Sun Tzu, *The Art of War***

Purchasing in your own name, in a company or through various other types of entities will result in very different rates of tax being paid. It is extremely important to get this right, as to move a property from one structure to another will generally result in transfer duty, which can be quite expensive. Sometimes you may need to use multiple entities due to the various concerns that can apply, like asset protection, negative gearing and various tax scenarios.

## Ownership annual net profit/loss

Let's use the example quoted earlier on the likely tax effect of a single property, as shown below:

**Figure 28 Tax effect on a single property**

| Item | $ |
|---|---|
| Purchase price | 1,000,000 |
| | |
| Rent income | 45,000 |
| Expenses | |
| Depreciation | 35,000 |
| Rates and taxes | 15,000 |
| Interest on loan | 60,000 |
| Repairs | 15,000 |
| Total expenses | 125,000 |
| | |
| Net loss | –80,000 |
| Tax benefit or refund at 47% | 37,600 |
| After-tax loss | –42,400 |
| Add back depreciation (non-cash item) | 35,000 |
| Net cash loss | –7,400 |

As an individual taxed at 47 per cent on your marginal income, the tax benefit is $37,600. If this property were to be held in a trust, there would be no tax benefit. The trust would show the loss and be able to offset it against future income. If the above were held in a company, the same would apply. In both examples (a trust or company), it could not distribute the loss to a person on a high salary to enable the tax benefit shown in Figure 28.

If, for example, the property started to make a profit, such as shown below, the tax payable on this profit under different structures would be as follows:

**Figure 29 Tax ramifications under different structures**

| Assume an annual profit | 50,000 |
| --- | --- |
| | |
| Tax payable as an individual | 23,500 |
| Tax payable if property is owned by a company | 15,000 |
| Tax payable if property is owned via a trust | 12,500 |
| Tax payable if property is owned in a super fund (in accumulation mode) | 7,500 |
| Tax payable if property is owned in a super fund (in pension mode) | 0 |

This is based on the following assumptions:

- The company only owns property and hence is a non-base rate (passive income) company and is taxed at 30 per cent on its profits.
- The trust has the ability to distribute to low-income beneficiaries under its discretionary trust provisions and hence reduce the tax payable by the beneficiaries to 25 per cent. If the beneficiaries had no other income they may be able to use the tax-free threshold of $18,200.

Therefore, when making a loss, the preferred ownership structure would be 100 per cent ownership by the person paying the highest marginal tax. When the property is making a profit, the preferred structure would be either a trust (family trust or unit trust) or your self-managed superannuation fund when it is in pension mode. As I said earlier, this isn't an easy choice.

## Capital gains on sale – under different structures

Let us now turn our attention to the tax payable on the sale of an investment property and the tax payable when the property is held in different structures. We will assume there are no carried forward capital losses from other property sales.

An important aspect of this is planning the sale event. Never enter a transaction without being aware of the impact of a sale. For example, if in a particular tax year you have a high income, it may be wise to defer any sales and hence capital gain realisations to a later year. If, for example, you are holding an asset that looks like it will realise a capital loss, you may wish to time the sale of any asset with a capital gain in the same year that you sell the asset with a capital loss. Be smart about this. Also be aware that the sale date, for tax purposes, is the date the sale contract goes unconditional, not the settlement date.

Let's assume the following sale scenario:

**Figure 30 Example sale scenario**

| Description and entity | $ |
|---|---|
| Purchase price | 500,000 |
| Legal fees stamp duty | 2,500 |
| Transfer/stamp duty | 16,000 |
| Improvements | 25,000 |
| | 543,500 |
| | |
| Sale price | 1,000,000 |
| Less agent's commission | 25,000 |
| Less legal fees | 1,500 |
| | 973,500 |
| | |
| Net profit | 430,000 |

The scenario in Figure 30 is an example of what could occur. This helps review what the tax effect may be. However, as mentioned earlier, do not sell a property without knowing the tax effect of a transaction and, such as in the example, setting aside the taxes that will be payable on this sale.

**Figure 31 Tax payable by an individual**

| | |
|---|---|
| Net profit as above | 430,000 |
| Less 50% CGT discount | 215,000 |
| Taxable gain | 215,000 |
| Tax payable as an individual | 101,050 |

If the property is held in joint names (say, a husband and wife or other family members), the tax in Figure 31 may be reduced with the use of income splitting. The net effect of this income splitting will be based on the tax thresholds of the person holding the share. If both are on high incomes and their marginal tax rate is 47 per cent, there will be no benefit.

**Figure 32 Tax payable if held in a trust**

| | |
|---|---|
| Net profit as above distributed to beneficiaries | 430,000 |
| Less 50% CGT discount | 215,000 |
| Taxable gain | 215,000 |
| Tax payable by beneficiaries | 53,750 |

**Figure 33 Tax payable if held in a company**

| | |
|---|---|
| Net profit as above | 430,000 |
| Less CGT discount | – |
| Taxable gain | 430,000 |
| Tax payable by a company | 129,000 |

**Figure 34 Tax payable if held in a super fund in accumulation mode**

| | |
|---|---|
| Net profit as above | 430,000 |
| Less CGT discount | – |
| Taxable gain | 430,000 |
| Tax payable by a super fund (10%) | 43,000 |

**Figure 35 Tax payable if held in a super fund in pension mode**

| | |
|---|---|
| Net profit as above | 430,000 |
| Less CGT discount | – |
| Taxable gain | 430,000 |
| Tax payable by a super fund | – |

From these examples, a super fund in pension mode wins, hands down. However, be aware of the rules surrounding superannuation funds, as covered later in the chapter. This is followed by a trust and then an individual taxpayer. The tax benefit of using a trust will only occur if there are beneficiaries in the trust that have low or no other income. A company structure loses out completely and is not the preferred option to own investment properties in.

This is why having a thorough understanding of the taxes payable by different entities and through different structures is vital. As mentioned earlier, sometimes situations change and what may work during one period in your wealth creation cycle may not work later. Be flexible. Consider your options but, more importantly, be proactive in making decisions. Following is a list with more detail on the tax rates that apply to various entities. Use this as a reference point, as often the detail can be very important in understanding the tax payable. For example, to obtain the CGT discount, you must be an Australian resident at the time of a sale.

## Individual tax rates

**Figure 36 Resident tax rates 2024–25**

| Taxable income | Tax on this income |
|---|---|
| $0–18,200 | Nil |
| $18,201–45,000 | 16c for each $1 over $18,200 |
| $45,001–135,000 | $4,288 plus 30c for each $1 over $45,000 |
| $135,001–190,000 | $31,288 plus 37c for each $1 over $135,000 |
| $190,001 and over | $51,638 plus 45c for each $1 over $190,000 |

The rates in Figure 36 do not include the Medicare levy of 2 per cent or the Medicare levy surcharge (MLS) of up to 1.5 per cent. All Australian residents are required to pay the Medicare levy, even if they have private health insurance. The MLS applies if you do not have private health insurance and your income is above $97,000 as an individual or $194,000 as a family. The surcharge rate starts at 1 per cent and increases to 1.5 per cent as your income increases to $151,000 as an individual and $301,000 as a family. Therefore, as an individual, your personal tax rate without private health insurance and in the highest tax bracket could be as high as 48.5 per cent.

## Company tax rates

The government introduced a two tax rate system for companies on 23 August 2018. This affected the rate of tax companies pay from the 2018 income year to the present. The terms 'base rate' and 'passive income' were introduced.

Loosely speaking, providing a company's passive income is not more than 80 per cent of its assessable income, the lower tax rate of 25 per cent will apply. Passive income includes rents, royalties, net capital gains, interest, dividends, and trust and partnership distributions. But, as always, the devil is in the detail and it is not quite as simple as it sounds. I have seen many situations where the finer detail of the definitions of passive income give a different outcome than expected. The definition of assessable income can also be important, as well as how you divide the assessable income based on the above information. The lower company tax rate applies to base rate entities with an aggregated turnover of less than $50 million.

If the only assets held in your company are rental properties, it will be difficult, if not impossible, to meet the less than 80 per cent rule, so it is more than likely the tax rate applicable, if your assets are held in a company, will be 30 per cent.

## Tax payable by superannuation funds

A complying superannuation fund pays tax at 15 per cent on both earnings and concessional (tax deductible to the payer) contributions received. This will apply while the fund is in accumulation mode.

When a super fund is in accumulation mode, capital gains are taxed at 10 per cent. When the fund moves to pension mode, the fund does not pay any tax on income earned. To confuse matters, the tax rate rules relate to the members rather than the fund. Of course, the fund pays the tax, which is then charged to the member's balance. One member can be in pension mode while other members can be in accumulation mode.

A member can have a pension account and an accumulation account, and still receive concessional contributions. In this case, the income will be apportioned across the pension balance and the accumulation balance. Tax at 15 per cent will only be payable on the accumulation portion of the income. If this situation arises, it is important to commute (transfer) any accumulation balance to an account-based pension (pension mode). This is an extremely easy process. I know the difference is minor (15% versus zero), but it should be done each year if the fund is still receiving concessional contributions. The aim will be to ensure that the fund pays the minimum tax possible. This will ensure all capital gains and profits earned are totally tax free. Yes, you read this right, totally tax free.

Superannuation has massive benefits on how you fund your future retirement. The system was introduced and continues to be used as a vehicle to shelter income and reduce tax. Many young people have trouble seeing the future benefit, as they tend to focus on a short timeframe. There is a lot of regulation surrounding superannuation because of these tax benefits. Also, you cannot access your superannuation balance until you meet a condition of release, which is generally when you retire or reach age 65. But do not be afraid to consider this option.

## Tax payable by trusts

This can also be a confusing area, although with research, it is not. Think of a trust as a flow-through entity. Unless you want the trust to be taxed at the top marginal tax rate (45% + 2% Medicare levy), a trust must flow (or distribute) all its profits to its beneficiaries. Hence, tax is levied to the beneficiaries at their marginal tax rates.

The trustee of the trust is required to decide on who it will distribute its net income to before 30 June each financial year. While at this time, the exact profit will not be known, the trust must, by a resolution or meeting minutes, state how the net profit for the year will be distributed to the beneficiaries of the trust. They must be listed and may, for example, simply receive a percentage of the net profit, a fixed amount with the balance being paid to a default beneficiary. Of course, from a tax-planning point of view, this will decide the most tax-effective manner in which the profit of the trust will be distributed.

The trust will set up a notional account for each beneficiary that it distributes income to. The notional account will have a balance that must eventually be paid to the beneficiary, otherwise it will create what is called an 'unpaid present entitlement' (UPE). If these UPEs are not discharged, they become a loan from the beneficiary to the trust. This loan if not repaid by the trust can cause further tax issues in later years. This is a complicated area that is still subject to tax law interpretation.

Trusts have benefits, but they do not suit every situation and there are traps to be careful of. The main disadvantage is that losses are trapped in a trust and cannot be distributed. You can also get UPE problems, as noted, if the profit is not actually paid to the beneficiary. The main advantage is that you can play the tax rate game more easily by paying profits to beneficiaries who fall in the lower tax rates.

Either discretionary trusts or unit trusts are the preferred option for holding investment property.

## Part 5

# Tax tips and the taxation aspects of property

Fortune favours the bold, sometimes you must take a risk.

**Latin proverb**

In this section we will get into the specifics of the Australian tax system and how it taxes property transactions. Some of this will be hard to follow and some aspects may not affect what you, the reader, intend to do. But these areas need to be covered, if only in a general way, to highlight any potential problems or risks.

I have already covered many of these throughout this book in general terms. Now we need to get specific. Sometimes, the devil is in the detail. For example, what date is applicable for capital gains purposes when you sell property? Is it the contract date or settlement date? The dates used for the holding period apply to gain the benefit of the 50 per cent CGT discount, the sole and principal residence exemptions and any overlap periods when you move from one principal place of residence to another. What is the GST impact on property sales and developments? How do the rollover relief provisions work? What is the order in which capital losses are applied, especially if you are able to use other concessions like the 50 per cent active asset test, 50 per cent small business test or rollover to a self-managed super fund of the balance of any gains?

The ATO does a great job in creating confusion on all of the above. There are strict timelines and strict criteria that can allow or deny a deduction, with massive financial consequences if you get it wrong.

## 22

# Using the tax system – a warning on intent or purpose

The hardest thing in the world to understand is income tax.

**Albert Einstein**

Many Australians, including myself, have an obsession with owning property. It continues to be the safest (in the long term) method of accumulating wealth. However, there are many different situations that can occur in life and a wide scope of various types of property transactions, from subdividing and selling off your backyard to more sophisticated taxpayers who carry on a business of property development.

The tax treatment of property transactions varies significantly depending on the intent of the taxpayer when the asset is acquired, and whether this is completed in your personal name, in a partnership, through a company, a unit trust or a discretionary trust. This will classify how the transaction will be treated for tax purposes, during its ownership or when it is eventually sold.

Basically, property transactions fall into three broad taxing categories:

1. Trading stock in the ordinary course of a property development business
2. Part of an isolated profit-making scheme or undertaking (referred to as a profit-making scheme)
3. A 'mere realisation of a capital asset'.

Be careful that property transactions are correctly characterised for income tax, GST and CGT purposes. Many people use property to create wealth, and so property transactions are always on the Australian Taxation Office's (ATO) radar. The ATO has data-matching arrangements with the land titles office to match and record all property sales and purchases. It also issued a taxpayer alert referred to as TA 2014/1 to warn taxpayers against the misclassification of profits arising from the sale of property.

While this is an extremely complicated area and the tax rulings and court cases could fill your entire office with paper, I will attempt to explain the three categories in a very simple way using an example.

Miss Red sees a property advertised for sale. It is on a large block and looks like it is capable of subdividing and maybe even building a second house. She investigates and it seems okay. She buys it, subdivides the block, builds a second house and then sells both houses. The tax situation will be categorised as the first point in the list, a profit-making development on revenue account. The sale of the original house will be GST free, but the sale of the new house will be subject to GST withholding, which will be paid directly to the ATO by the buyer on the sale. The GST payable will be based on the sale price (at 10%), but the seller will be able to claim back the input credits on the construction costs. The net

GST will more than likely be around 7 per cent of the sale price of the second home. In respect of the realisation of both homes, if we assume Miss Red makes a $2 million profit and the acquisition is in her personal name, she will be taxed on the full $2 million profit at her marginal tax rate. Tax payable will be in the order of $940,000 (47%). GST will also be payable.

Consider that Mr Black sees this same property and thinks it could be a good investment. He purchases it, rents the first house and builds the second house. He is not sure what he will do with it as he hasn't decided when he would sell. He thinks that, in the long term, it will be a good investment and thinks he will hold both properties for investment purposes. Because he hasn't sold the new house, no GST will be applicable. If he rents it out and holds it for four years, it will be GST free. If he ever sells either of the two houses, he will avail himself of the 50 per cent CGT discount. So, in this example and assuming a profit of $2 million on one house, as an individual, tax would be payable on $1 million at 47 per cent, equalling $470,000.

In a third scenario, assume Mrs White looks at this property. She thinks she will live in the house. It has a great backyard for her family and certainly some upside potential. She buys it, lives in it as her sole and principal residence. She thinks one day her children will leave home and the house will be too big for her and her partner, so she investigates building a new house on the back lot. Council take forever to approve it, but after about five years it is all sorted. She builds the second house, sells the original house and moves into the new house at the back. In this situation, the first house is her sole and principal residence, so no tax is payable when it is sold. If and when she sells the new house, again this will be her sole and principal residence and also tax free. The entire exercise, if handled correctly, will be totally tax free for Mrs White.

Be mindful of the overlap periods that apply. But you can see how adjusting your lifestyle to meet the tax consequences can be extremely rewarding. In these examples, Miss Red pays $940,000 in tax (plus GST), Mr Black pays $470,000 and Mrs White pays no tax.

## Part IVA

No chapter on the intent and purpose associated with the purchase of a property would be complete without an explanation of Part IVA of the *Income Tax Assessment Act 1936*. Basically, Part IVA is a catch-all section that says if the dominant purpose of a transaction is to save tax, then that taxation deduction will be denied. The section was introduced in 2005 and improved in 2013 to catch blatant, artificial and contrived schemes that had no basis other than to save tax. For transactions to be caught under this section of the Act, three characteristics must be present:

1. There must be a 'scheme', which broadly means any actions or transactions. This would allow the ATO to consider various tax schemes put forward by various tax promotors.
2. There must be a 'tax benefit' that flows as a result of entering into the above scheme; hence, some form of financial advantage in entering into the transaction or scheme.

3. The dominant purpose is to obtain a tax benefit. When the facts are reviewed, including the way the transaction is structured and its financial implications, the main purpose must be to obtain a tax benefit.

In the early 1990s, it was common around May or June for various promotors to come up with schemes that, in effect, would reduce the taxes payable on profits made in a particular year. Many of these were extremely blatant and contrived; frankly, they deserved to be legislated against. For example, bottom of the harbour schemes would basically scuttle a company that had massive unrealised profits by appointing new 'straw' directors (sometimes homeless people) and letting the company go into liquidation with no assets available to be sold to pay the tax debts. Other schemes were less blatant, but nonetheless designed to eliminate all taxes payable via clever 'round robin' transactions.

To not be subject to Part IVA, the dominate purpose must be some other reason, other than tax saving. For example, an asset is purchased for future income reasons. Yes, there may be some initial tax benefit, but the dominant purpose might be to create an income stream sufficient to retire on.

## How to ensure Part IVA is not an issue

Keep all documentation that will substantiate a commercial reason for the purchase. The presence of your commercial reason is crucial in defending any Part IVA claims. Document the other reasons and motivations behind a purchase, like asset protection or family income independence, and all and any non-tax objectives associated with a purchase.

Make sure the arrangement is aligned with the intent previously described. Of course, tax planning is allowed, but you must ensure that your strategy is not dominated by a tax-saving purpose.

Don't be afraid to talk to the ATO if unsure. The ATO has emphasised the importance of engagement, particularly concerning intangible assets and digital transactions. There are some principles outlined in a taxpayer alert 2018/2 that deal with a few grey areas. These are around timing, investment, CGT discounts and trading digital assets being treated as trading stock.

Keep an eye on any changes to the legislation or court cases dealing with this. Some set precedents either in the taxpayer's favour or in the ATO's favour and sometimes clarify how the ATO would treat certain transactions. It can help avoid compliance risks if you are audited.

# 23

# Tax tip 1 – your sole and principal residence (don't lose the concession)

For most Australians, this will be your biggest tax haven. I know you may not think of it that way, but the truth is that there is no tax payable on any gains you make on your family home. For this reason, you should put a lot of effort into creating an asset that increases in value. The net effect will be a retirement nest egg that may pay for your retirement when you downsize to something smaller or even move to a retirement home.

Statistically, based on a survey by Finder in 2024, 2.8 million Australians have a net worth over $1 million. The number that are millionaires because of the value of their home only and excluding other investments is 1.7 million. This is the number of people who have become wealthy solely based on the value of their home.

There is no reason why you cannot use this tax-free status to grow your asset base. Do not be content with buying a house and sitting on it for 30 years. Continually upgrade your position, renovate, improve, sell, buy again and do the same.

This will usually be the first step in wealth creation. Building equity in your sole and principal residence allows you to borrow to purchase more assets, income-producing assets that will grow your asset base over time.

Following are some case studies on how this has worked for myself and people I know. These case studies illustrate how they have set out to use the tax-free status of their PPR to build wealth. I've also included some traps to be careful of.

In 1979, my wife and I purchased a house in Earlwood in Sydney's inner west. We paid $26,000 for that house. It needed a new kitchen and bathroom, as well as some external landfill to level the block. We spent around $15,000 on renovations. We sold that house in about 1985 for $85,000, a profit of $34,000. We purchased our next house in Belrose on the Northern Beaches, paying $106,000. We spent around $50,000 on it, selling it in 1993 for $350,000, a profit of $194,000. We bought and sold a few properties in between, but then settled on a house at Bayview, which we acquired for $690,000 (debt free). This house was in need of a lot of work. Renovations had started but the previous owner had run out of money. Again, it needed a new kitchen, two new bathrooms and extensive groundworks. After over ten years and almost $350,000 in renovation costs, we completed it. We eventually sold it in 2010 for $1.8 million. A profit of over $750,000. All tax free.

We had a neighbour in Belrose who was the local butcher. His business did not make much money, but he was able to accumulate wealth by doing the exact same thing. Every two years, he would buy and sell, renovating for a profit each time. He effectively ratcheted himself up using these gains to buy bigger and better homes that became debt free due to the profits he made. All gains made were tax free because, on all occasions, each house was his sole and principal residence.

On this point, be careful about your intention. If the sole intention is somewhere to live and ancillary to this is making a profit on any future sale, then you will not run afoul of the ATO 'flipping' rules. After all, people sell their homes for many reasons, some of which have nothing to do with tax.

I know the strategies used in these case studies may require renovation work. I know, for some, the thought of renovating where you live is uncomfortable and inconvenient. It can also sometimes be disruptive and mean sacrifice for your family when you are constantly doing renovations. I suggest you try and limit the disruption by doing the most disruptive renovations (like kitchens and bathrooms) before you move in. But, as noted, the rewards can be high and because the gains are tax free, they are even better.

On the sole and principal residence exemptions, be careful that you do not lose this exemption. You can only have one sole and principal residence at any point in time. Holiday homes or weekenders do not qualify. If you own more than one property, you need to select which property will be treated as your sole and principal residence. If any of the following exemptions apply, you must make this choice in the income year that you first sell one of these properties. The capital gain on the sale of your sole and principal residence will be exempt and hence tax free if you are an Australian resident and the property:

- has been the home of your partner and other dependants for the whole period you have owned it; and

- has not been used to produce income – that is, you have not run a business from it, rented it out or purchased it with the intention to 'flip' it (bought it to renovate and sell at a profit); and
- is on land of 2 hectares or less.

There are some exemptions that can apply to this, depending on your situation:

- If you move into a new house, your new home is generally exempt from CGT from the time you acquire it. This time period is based on the settlement date of the contract (not the contract date, as is the case for investment property CGT time periods).
- If there is a delay in moving in because of illness or other unforeseen circumstances, your home is still exempt, provided you move in as soon as the cause of the delay is removed (eg when you recover from the illness).
- If you cannot move in because the property is being rented to someone, the property does not become your main residence until you move in. This rental period will create a CGT event when you sell the property.
- If you have not yet sold your former home, you can treat both homes as your main residence for up to 6 months. You can only do this if you satisfy all of the following requirements:
  - Your old home was your main residence for a continuous period of at least three months in the 12 months before you disposed of it.

  - You did not use your old home to produce income (such as rent) in any part of that 12 months when it was not your main residence.
  - The new property becomes your main residence.
- If you move out of your home, you can continue treating your former home as your main residence even if you rent it out (the six-year rule). These rules are complicated and there is a six-month duplication period. The following must apply:
  - The property must have been your main residence first. You can't apply the main residence exemption to a period before a property first becomes your main residence (eg if you rented out your home before you lived in it, the main residence exemption doesn't apply to the period you rented out your home).
  - You stop living in it.
  - You cannot have another house as your sole and principal residence during this time. Generally, the person would move out and relocate for work reasons to some other area and rent a house. If you purchased another house and moved into it, the six-year rule will cease on the date you settle the new house.
  - The six-year rule does not need to be a continuous six years. It could be broken up with, say, six years vacant and four years rented. In this case, the entire ten years is CGT free.
  - If the home is rented for more than six years, the excess period will be subject to CGT. You should

obtain an independent valuation on the date the six-year rule ends and use this value as the cost base to calculate the capital gain for CGT purposes.

- If you use your home for rental purposes or to run a business, you will not get the full main residence exemption and may need to obtain a valuation to calculate the home's market value at the time you first used it for business purposes or rented it. If you don't, you can use the days of ownership versus the days it is rented and apportion the gain accordingly. I recommend you obtain a valuation when the home becomes a rental property or starts being used for business purposes. That will give you the option to calculate the CGT payable using both methods. Then you can choose the method that will result in the lowest CGT payable.
- If part of your home is used for business purposes, you will need to calculate (using a square metre method) the portion or percentage of your home that is used for business purposes. That portion of your home will no longer be treated as your sole and principal residence. It will be that portion that will be subject to any capital gains tax.
- If you live in a different home to your spouse or children, you need to choose which home will be your main residence.
- If you build or renovate your home on land you own, you can treat the land as your main residence for up to four years before you move in, provided you move in as soon as practicable after it is finished.

- If you lose your home because it is destroyed or compulsorily acquired, generally the main residence exemption will still apply.
- If your home is on more than 2 hectares of land, only 2 hectares can be CGT exempt. You should obtain a valuation of the exempt and non-exempt portions.
- If you leave Australia and become a non-resident of Australia, all capital gains will be subject to tax. You lose the tax-free period that the sole and principal residence was used as a home. To me, this is extremely unfair as in effect the ATO is backdating the sole and principal residence exemption. If you intend on moving overseas, you should sell your principal place of residence before you move, even if you use these proceeds to buy an investment property. That way, the sole and principal residence CGT exemption will be crystallised for the period the property was your home and not lost completely.
- If you demolish your house and sell your principal place of residence as vacant land, you are not entitled to the main residence exemption because, quite simply, you cannot live on a vacant block of land. Because there is no dwelling on the land, when it is sold, you cannot claim a partial exemption for the period that the land had a dwelling on it and it was used as your sole and principal residence. Don't fall into this trap if you are contemplating selling your property to a property developer. If you are contemplating this or undertaking a subdivision and selling as vacant lots, the main residence exemption will only be available

if the sale occurs while a dwelling that is your main residence remains on the land you sell. If you decide to rebuild after demolishing the house, the main residence exemption can still be claimed if:

- you make an election to treat the vacant land as your main residence from the time the demolished house was last occupied by you; and
- there is no more than four years between the time of last occupation of the demolished dwelling and the time the new house becomes your main residence.

If you meet the conditions listed above, you do not pay tax on any capital gain when you sell your home and you ignore any capital loss. From the above, there are some partial exemptions if you do not meet all these conditions. But be careful, as some trigger points can result in a loss of the entire exemption and tax being payable on a sale.

If you are contemplating any of the above, be very careful to obtain professional help. These rules are tricky and onerous. In some cases, you will need to obtain a valuation when there is a change in use. This will set the new cost base for capital gains purposes.

I have seen many cases where what might logically seem like the case is actually not. For example, you have a home in Australia for a long period of time and then take a job overseas. Logic dictates that the period of ownership while living in Australia should be tax free, but it is not. I have seen taxpayers caught with massive capital gains tax that could have been avoided if they had better advice.

# 24

# Tax tip 2 – duplex and subdivision

A great way to create wealth is to buy a house to live in that is on a large block of land that in time may be capable of subdivision. A worked example of this is mentioned earlier in this book; however, nothing stops you from buying an investment property and building two homes on it, whether that involves demolishing one house or incorporating the original house into the development. As we have explored the first option elsewhere, let's consider the second option in more detail.

Before we consider this, remember that capital gains are only realised when you sell. In this case, there will be CGT and GST implications.

If you purchase an investment property on a large block of land and build a second house (retaining the first house), you are creating a new asset. This asset will be created when the titles to the subdivision are registered with the land titles office. If both houses are rented, then CGT will apply when they are sold. But what base do you use? The first purchase consisted of an old house and a block of land. The subdivision is the land component only. You will need to calculate the value of the newly created block of land by apportioning the original cost. For example, if the large block of land with one house on it cost $1 million, the old house might be worth $250,000. The balance of the land could be $750,000. If the subdivided portion was 33 per cent of the total land area, then the land component of the new block would have a cost base of $250,000. A valuer should be used for this. Then, if you build a new house on the new block, that build cost will be added to the land component cost. If you sell the newly created house and land, two taxes will be payable. Firstly, as you have created a new asset, GST will be payable. This will be based on 1/11th of the sale price. However, you will be able to offset this GST collected from the buyer against GST paid on construction. To do this, you would need to register for GST and obtain an ABN (in the same way you would if you are carrying on a business). On settlement, the buyer is required to pay the GST to the ATO (not to you, the seller). You must then lodge a business activity statement (BAS), declaring the GST paid on construction costs, legal fees and even agent's commission, called input credits. When you prepare and lodge your BAS, you should elect to use what is referred to as the margin scheme. This allows an input credit on all costs except the land component. More than likely, when you purchased the property you did not pay GST. You will then receive a refund based on the GST at 1/11th of the sale price less the input credits mentioned above. This is a complicated area, and you should use a professional to assist with this.

When you lodge your income tax return for the year, capital gains tax will be payable on the difference between the cost base (which includes the land component and build costs) and the net sale price after GST. It would be hard to argue that this development was carried out for any other purpose than to make a profit. Hence, as a profit-making scheme, you would not be able to claim the 50 per cent CGT discount.

The main theme behind this book is how to create a property portfolio for long-term rental income and future capital gains. To not be subject to GST, an investment property needs to be rented (or available for rent) for a continuous period of at least five years from completion date. This is the date titles are issued to the date a sale contract is entered into. It cannot be less than five years, as the rental period must be at least five years or GST will be payable. The period must be continuous, which also means that if the period was broken because you lived in the premises as your sole and principal residence, the five-year rule will not apply.

To obtain the CGT discount of 50 per cent, an investment property must be acquired for long-term rental and owned for a minimum of 12 months. The purchase date is the date of the contract (when purchased) or the date the asset was created where it is a new asset. The sale date again is the contract date, not the settlement date.

There is an additional CGT discount of up to 10 per cent for individuals who are Australian residents for tax purposes who provide affordable rental housing to people earning low to moderate income. This increases the CGT discount to up to 60 per cent for owners of these residential rental properties.

# 25

# Tax tip 3 – selling off your backyard

Selling a portion of your sole and principal residence is similar to Tax tip 2 on creating a duplex. The main difference is that part of the land that is now to be subdivided and sold off was originally tax free and part of your sole and principal residence. I have covered some of these points earlier, but they are worth repeating, if only in a more simplistic manner, but with a few more twists that you need to be aware of. In other words, I will explain how to play this game in the most tax-effective manner.

You could subdivide your property, build a new house on the subdivided portion and then sell your existing house and move into the new house. Providing you did that within six months of the titles being issued, both houses would be free from capital gains tax and free from GST.

The other option is that you could rent the new house. Providing you retain the rented house for 12 months, you will get the 50 per cent CGT discount. But GST will be payable, unless you rent it for a continuous period of at least five years (see Tax tip 2).

The ATO considers that your intent is vital in deciding whether the subdivision of your backyard is a profit-making scheme, and hence taxable without any CGT discounts. Using ATO terminology on revenue account rather than on capital account, common examples where a transaction is to be treated as a profit-making scheme are the following:

- You acquire a property with the intention of constructing two townhouses that will be sold on completion.
- You subdivide your backyard and build a house on the vacant land that will be sold upon completion.

It would be obvious that in both of these situations, the intent is clear. The transactions are both on revenue account and hence taxable in full, with no discounts. They clearly are not on capital account, which is defined as a 'mere realisation of a capital asset', because the developments involve the intent to construct two dwellings and to sell them for a profit.

For this transaction not to be treated as a profit-making scheme, there needs to be other considerations. This may be a new house to live in or creating an additional rental property to give you extra income. That changes the character of the transaction and hence you escape the ATO's treatment that will make all gains fully taxable. The other word of warning is your original intent on acquisition. According to the ATO, it is very difficult for taxpayers to abandon an initial profit-making intention after acquisition of the land so as to convert a revenue asset into a capital one. For example, suppose you acquire land for the purposes of building residential units for sale, but then you subsequently decide not to sell the units and instead to retain the units for rental purposes. Perhaps the market is flat or the price expectation is too high. Suppose you hold them for many years (more than five). On the sale of a unit or units, the ATO would likely argue the profit arose as part of a profit-making scheme; that is, the disposal would be more than a mere realisation of a capital asset. There has been a lot of controversy about this but be aware the ATO may make your life hard if you say too much to others, like your bank, and then change your mind. There have even been a number of court cases that have resulted in very mixed decisions.

When does the backyard subdivision cross over from being a profit-making scheme (fully taxable) to being a mere realisation of a capital asset and hence subject to the concessions noted earlier? How can you ensure the latter applies? The answer to this is a matter of the fact and manner in which the realisation occurred. It inevitably involves, firstly, whether the land was acquired for a profit-making purpose and, secondly, the degree of activity involved (and the taxpayer's involvement therein).

## Granny flat arrangements

The ATO recognises that sometimes you may wish to create an additional dwelling for a family member (for example, a granny flat). Providing you meet the criteria below and there is a written agreement that will give an individual the right to occupy a property for life, no capital gains tax applies for arrangements that commence from 1 July 2021. No CGT is payable when a granny flat arrangement is created, varied or terminated.

To be exempt from CGT, in accordance with the ATO guidelines, a granny flat arrangement must:

- be in writing
- indicate an intention that the parties are legally bound
- not be a commercial arrangement. As such it cannot be based on market rent, but contributions to household costs such as electricity, water and rates are okay

It should include:

- the parties involved in the arrangement, including the individual(s) with an ownership interest in the property
- the circumstances in which the arrangement can be varied or terminated
- what happens when the arrangement is varied or terminated.

A granny flat arrangement can be entered into with any party, including family or friends. Be aware that sometimes land tax and additional council rates may be payable.

26

# Tax tip 4 - rental properties (on acquisition and sale)

This should be the second plank in building your wealth. After you have built equity in your sole and principal residence, you can now look at buying your first investment asset class. This may be the start of a share portfolio, or a property portfolio. I make no comment on what is the best investment that you should make as everyone's situation is different. To make it easier, in this chapter I will cover the acquisition of your first rental property.

While I am sure most would be familiar with the rental property rules and concessions, it is useful to recount these to ensure you don't miss or forget what is available. Sometimes the devil is in the detail, so don't miss something because you get a small aspect wrong (like ownership structure). There are two areas that are covered in this chapter. First, the tax tips and tax benefits associated with the holding of rental properties. The second relates to the concessions available on their sale.

## Holding investment property – the tax concessions

These fall into two broad areas. The first is the negative gearing aspect. This is where the holding costs exceed the rental income. The second is the non-cash effect of depreciation claims, both of which have a very positive effect on the tax you pay.

The best way to explain this is with an example. Assume your annual rent from your property is $25,000 per annum. Then assume that during the year, you incur interest costs, rates, body corporate fees and some repairs that total, say, $27,000. Your net cash loss is $2000 per annum. No big deal and easy to cover. But here is where it gets interesting. If you purchased a new or relatively new property, you could expect to claim depreciation write-offs. You will need to obtain a depreciation report from a licensed quantity surveyor to calculate the amount that is claimable. This report will usually cost around $700. Let's assume the deprecation claimable is $8000. Now your loss for tax purposes is $10,000. If you are at the top marginal tax bracket, this will give rise to a tax refund of $4700. The tax refund has more than paid the cash flow shortfall.

This formula holds true for all rental properties held. Hence, you can see why professionals such as doctors, lawyers and even accountants own multiple properties – sometimes ten or more. They are using their rental properties to reduce their current tax and build wealth for the future. Of course, wealth is only built when the properties go up in value. Over time, this is generally true. I personally have a preference for new units, as there is no maintenance, depreciation is higher and the management of the tenants can be handled by onsite managers. This is a personal preference, and you must decide what is right for you.

When you sell a property, all depreciation claims will need to be returned as income because you have now recouped that depreciation. Hence, depreciation is only a timing difference that allows a write-off that is eventually returned on the sale of the property if the sale price is more than the cost price, which it will be over time.

The other point that can be useful, which is discussed later, is that holding property can assist with one-off tax planning. Assume, in a year, that you have a large capital gain or a large income for some reason that may not recur. This gain (and the tax associated with it) can be offset or completely eliminated by simply prepaying one year's interest on one or more of your property loans. On 29 June, you borrow and pay in advance the next year's interest on a loan associated with your income-earning properties. This will be deductible in the year it is paid. Your tax bill can be reduced accordingly. I have personally done this a number of times.

Just a point on interest and tax deductibility, which I have seen clients get wrong. The rule is that a tax deduction is based on what the money is used for, rather than the security used to obtain the loan. I had a client that repaid his rental property loan and then did a redraw to upgrade the house he lived in. The bank security was on the rental property, but the money was used for his personal residence. He felt the above was logical, which it sort of was. He thought he was simply repaying the loan he made by taking back the money he used to repay the loan. But the fact is the interest on this redraw was not tax deductible.

If you want to reduce your debt levels, you should repay any non-deductible loans first (like on your home or personal cars) and retain the tax deductible loans. In respect of redraws, if the money is used to, say, renovate the rental property kitchen or build a pool in the rental property, then the interest will be tax deductible. If it is used for private purposes (as stated above), it will not be deductible. For example, you may have a home loan of $500,000 but a limit of $1 million on the facility. This may have been because you have been diligent in paying it off. If you use this redraw facility to purchase a rental property for $500,000, the interest portion of the loan (50%) would be tax deductible. As you make repayments on your home loan, both the deductible and non-deductible portion will be reduced proportionately. Just be careful with this one, as time and various other loan movements can make it tricky to calculate the deductible portion, especially in, say, 20 years' time. It is always best to split the loan and keep the deductible and non-deductible portions separate.

Similar to this, I have seen problems with borrowing the money in the wrong entity. For example, suppose you are purchasing a property in a unit trust. Strictly speaking, if you borrowed the money in your own name and then lent it to the unit trust, you could charge the unit trust the same or a similar interest to what you are paying. For example, you could invoice the unit trust each month, receive the money into your account and pay the loan interest. The ATO has a ruling on this that states there must be a commercial purpose for this arrangement. That purpose or reason may be that the bank would not lend the trust sufficient funds to enable the purpose to occur. To cover this, you may put a small margin on the amount charged and hence show a profit at your end. All very complicated but achievable, especially if you have an asset protection reason to encumber your own personal assets. The problem is a future problem. If the loan is a principal and interest loan, your cash flow will be an issue meeting the principal reductions. Then, as time goes by, the principal will be reduced and perhaps eliminated. Therefore, you cannot on-charge anything to the trust for this loan, as it no longer exists. The other issue is that if you wish to refinance, you may have a problem with the original use of funds and losing the tax deduction. We had a client whose previous accountant used this structure for asset protection reasons. Then 20 years later, the ATO queried the interest claim. The client could not substantiate what the original loan was used for. It had been refinanced a few times, sometimes with a different bank. The client couldn't remember which loan related to which properties. The bank was unable to help, as the records were too old. The ATO denied the interest claim. Frankly, it is better and easier to keep the loan in the entity that owns the asset. While there may be additional security, the interest claim will always be able to be substantiated.

## Tax concessions on the sale of rental property

The tax office allows a 50 per cent CGT exemption for any gains made on the sale of a rental property held for more than 12 months. This holding rule time period applies from the date a contract becomes unconditional. For example, if you purchase a property on 1 June with a 28-day finance clause, in 14 days, your loan is approved, and you advise the vendor. The date of purchase for CGT purposes will be 15 June. The same applies on the sale. The date will be when the contract to the buyer becomes unconditional. The 12-month holding rules are based on these dates. I have seen many cases where the client thought the settlement dates for the purchase and sale were used to ascertain whether the property was held for 12 months. While this may sound logical, as ownership is based on settlement, this is not the case from a tax perspective. If you have not held a rental property for in excess of 12 months, you do not get the 50 per cent CGT discount.

Consider the following example, assuming the holding rule has been satisfied:

**Figure 37 Example of tax consequences on the sale of a rental property**

| Description | $ |
|---|---|
| Sale price of property | $750,000 |
| Less: agent's commission and advertising costs | $18,500 |
| Less: legal fees on the sale | $2,500 |
| Net sale proceeds | $729,000 |
| Cost of property | $500,000 |
| Legal fees, stamp duty, etc. | $35,000 |
| Renovations and improvements | $85,000 |
| Total cost of property | $620,000 |
| Net profit | $109,000 |
| Less 50% CGT exemption | $54,500 |
| Taxable capital gain | $54,500 |

You have made $109,000 in profit. Now comes the tricky part. In Figure 37, we have a taxable capital gain (of $54,500) that is added to your taxable income and taxed at your marginal tax rate. The following scenarios will apply to this gain. If you plan your affairs, you should be able to choose the scenario that has the lowest tax option:

1. If the property is owned in both your and your spouse's name, then only $27,250 will be added to each of your taxable income for the year.

2. If you limit your income in the year the gain is made, the marginal tax will be lower. For example, if $27,250 is the only income both yourself and your spouse will earn in a year, the tax will be $1,720.00 × 2 = $3,440.00. If the profit is earned by one person, the tax will be $8,180.00.
3. If you are operating your business (hence your other income) through a company, you may be able to do the above by simply reducing the salary you pay yourself in the year the capital gain is made – drawings can be treated as a complying division 7A loan and not a salary.
4. If the above property is owned by a company, which we will assume is not a base rate entity (as the income is passive rent income), then the tax payable will be at 30 per cent on $109,000, which is a total of $32,700. Companies do not get the 50 per cent CGT discount. This is a very important tax-planning tip. Don't own real estate in a company structure. If the company is a base rate entity (because it trades and more than 80% of it is income from that trading), tax will be at 25 per cent and hence $27,250.
5. If you own other assets that have unrealised capital losses, it may pay to realise those losses in the same year.
6. If you cannot achieve any of the above, tax will be payable at the top marginal rate of 45 per cent, plus the Medicare levy of 2 per cent, totalling 47 per cent. Hence, you pay tax of $25,615.

Again, by planning and being proactive, you can limit the tax payable on the above gain. The point is that you have made a profit of $109,000 on the sale of this property and will pay tax anywhere from $3440 to $25,615 (or $32,700 if owned in a company structure, which I never recommend).

Your after-tax profit will range from $105,560 to $83,385. Still a good result!

The 50 per cent CGT exemption on rental properties is something many investors can benefit from. As a taxpayer, you need to ensure you meet all of the conditions and apply this concession to reduce your tax.

The above holds true for all assets that are purchased. Many people purchase a share portfolio using the same formula. I have seen massive gains from this, and I have seen massive losses. Shares can be more volatile in the short term, but in fact, in the long term, if you get it right, shares can increase in value more than property. As mentioned earlier, when the Commonwealth Bank listed, the shares were less than $9.00 each. They are now in excess of $150.00 per share and yield around 6 per cent as a fully franked dividend.

It is not the purpose of this book to review various investment options, but merely to point out the tax-planning tips associated with whatever strategy you choose. The main point is that you actually follow a strategy, that you are proactive in doing something about building wealth in a tax-effective way. These tips show you how this can be done and how to use the system to your advantage with property or shares. It's all totally legal and totally within the tax framework.

27

# Tax tip 5 – rental properties (ongoing tax claims)

What is claimable and not claimable in respect of rental properties? Sometimes, you need to be clever in how you do things; follow the rules, but use them to your advantage. In other words, change the transaction to make it tax effective, if you can. But be aware of the tax rules regarding intent and purpose and be aware of Part IVA of the Taxation Act dealing with schemes where the dominant purpose is to avoid tax. These are covered in Chapter 22.

Every year, the ATO comes out with scare tactics to warn property owners not to cheat the system. In fact, to ensure taxpayers don't make any mistakes (either purposely or by accident, in not knowing the rules), the ATO intends to double the number of 'in-depth' audits (to an estimated 4500) in 2024–2025.

The ATO noted that, in 2018, over 2.2 million taxpayers claimed over $47 billion in rental property related deductions. Hence, the ATO sees rental property claims as a major revenue risk. They also reported that as a result of a recent audit activity, nine out of ten of the returns contained errors. From 1500 rental property audits conducted in 2018, penalties totalling $1.3 million were raised. Therefore, don't take the risk of making claims that are unsupported.

The following are key areas where errors are often made. I know because I have seen it many times and corrected claims that would have resulted in problems for clients. These include the following:

- **Ensuring interest deductions are being claimed correctly.** As mentioned earlier, interest claims must be aligned to the purpose for which the loan was taken and not be for private purposes. Detailed examples of this were explained in Chapter 26. One point that does need clarifying is that an individual claims interest on a paid (cash) basis. This means when physically paid out of your bank account or charged on your loan statement. Your payments on your loan are not the amounts you can claim, it is only the interest portion. Therefore, it is often wise to use an interest-only loan for rental properties and a principal and interest loan on your sole and principal residence. Make any extra repayments on your home loan and not your rental properties. If you intend to make a prepayment of interest, you must get the bank to charge this to you and then pay it. Simply making an extra payment will not work. Be careful that you think about the funds needed to acquire a property and how best to maximise the tax deduction. Borrow the maximum amount needed rather than subsidise a loan with your own money, especially if you still owe money on your home loan. Sometimes, when you are purchasing your third or fourth property, you will have unused equity in your other properties. By maxing out the new loan, you are able to increase the tax claims.

- **Whether amounts claimed as repairs are associated with the rental property and are not of a capital nature.** Repairs must be restoring the original nature of the property and not an improvement. The biggest trap is initial repairs that are needed to bring a property up to a reasonable standard. These initial repairs are part of your cost base and are not deductible against rent received. They can't be, as you didn't have a tenant that caused the repair problems. However, if you have a property that is rented for, say, five years, and normal wear and tear applies, repairs will be claimable to bring the property back to either its original state or to a reasonable standard. Be careful about the distinction between a repair and an improvement. There are many tax cases on what constitutes a repair and what constitutes an improvement. An improvement is not deductible and may be either a capital cost that is added to the cost base of the property, like a new roof, or an asset that is depreciated over time, like a new kitchen or new carpet. For example, to replace a rotten deck may be a repair. To replace it with a different structure, like an enclosed patio or a massive extension, would be an improvement. In respect of repairs needed when you purchase a property, you may wish to only do minimal initial repairs and leave any larger repairs to later. After all, the new tenants may do more damage.
- **Depreciation claims for capital works.** These are depreciation claims associated with the building, including structural elements such as walls, floors and

the roof. Properties built before 16 September 1987 are not eligible for capital works deductions. For properties built after 15 September 1987, depreciation at the rate of 2.5 per cent per annum of the eligible cost is claimable.

- **Depreciation claims for plant and equipment.** This includes items such as carpets, ovens and blinds. Deductions are only available for new assets or items purchased directly by you. Depreciation cannot be claimed for second-hand plant and equipment in properties purchased after 9 May 2017. Depreciation of plant and equipment is based on the effective life of each asset. This will range from 15 to 33 per cent. If you purchase a new property or do a major renovation, you can arrange a quantity surveyor to prepare a depreciation report that will state the depreciation claims that can be made each year.
- **Other costs like council and water rates, body corporate fees, agent commissionand advertising for tenants.** In a cruel twist, the government removed the claims for travel costs incurred after 1 July 2017. Travel costs include car expenses, airfare, taxi, hire car, public transport, accommodation and meals, and may relate to costs incurred to collect rent, inspect a property or attend to repairs. Under section 8.1 of the *Income Tax Assessment Act 1997*, costs necessarily incurred in the gaining or producing of assessable income are stated as being deductible. However, by legislation, the government has specifically excluded any claims for travel costs incurred after 1 July 2017.

- If you have a holiday home, generally you are unable to claim any costs associated with it. If you rent it (at market rates and not at a discount to family or friends), costs associated with this rental will be deductible. For example, if you rent it for six months of the year, then 50 per cent of all costs will be deductible. If you rent it at a discount, you are required to take up the market rent as income and not the discounted rent.

If you receive rent from any online platforms, like Airbnb or any other arrangement, you are required to declare that rent as income. It is taxable, as is all income earned.

The number one reason stated by the ATO that claims are not allowed when an audit is done is because the person cannot support a claim with either receipts or some form of acceptable documentation. The ATO also made an additional warning that furnishing fraudulent or doctored records will attract higher penalties (and possibly prosecution).

It pays to be diligent in your record-keeping. Keep your receipts and keep all documentation in relation to your purchase and sale (if applicable). You must keep your records on the purchase (and sale) for five years after you sell your property. Unfortunately, if a property is your sole and principal residence and you rent it at a later date, you must have records associated with the purchase (and also any improvements), even though initially you had no intention of renting it. This will be needed to calculate the portion of CGT payable when you sell the property.

Besides classification issues, be aware that you must be able to support all of your claims. Interest is the biggest claim rental property owners incur, and this is the area that the ATO tends to focus on. This is an area that must be handled correctly. Ensure you review the common traps taxpayers make on this and avoid them.

In respect of other claims made, ensure you have documentation to substantiate the claim, such as a receipt and proof that you made the payment. I recall that in the past, many tradies would scour the floor of Bunnings to collect receipts for tools and items that they never actually purchased. They couldn't substantiate payment via a credit card or other means, and if audited would more than likely be prosecuted. Today, with online bookkeeping systems, this process is far easier. Bank feeds from your bank account or credit cards, email or scans of receipts direct into your accounting system make record-keeping so much easier. It will solve any recording issues in a future audit or review by the ATO. Just be careful that you make a back-up copy into a PDF format, in case at a later date you cancel your subscription to your bookkeeping system.

28

# Tax tip 6 – tax deductions on vacant land

The ATO has made tax deductions on vacant land a very complicated area to get right. Also, unfortunately, there are some traps that can catch taxpayers unexpectedly and unintentionally. I have attempted to explain them in a simple way, but it is hard, as so many different situations can occur. The bottom line is that, since 2019, claiming holding costs while you do a development or rebuild a rental property may not be possible. It is even the case that income received on land rented while you develop it will be taxable, yet the holding costs will not.

In October 2019, the ATO implemented provisions aimed at limiting income tax deductions for 'vacant land'. This is defined as any land upon where there is no eligible substantial and permanent structure erected upon it.

These rules will seriously impact cash flows, particularly when the intention is to construct or substantially renovate a rental property and/or business premises. When the land is vacant as defined above, the holding costs such as interest, rates, insurance, land tax and maintenance costs, which have been previously deductible, are no longer deductible if, at the time they are incurred, there is no eligible substantial and permanent structure on the land (subject to a number of exceptions). Of course, a way to handle this is to not demolish the existing dwelling until absolutely necessary.

These rules apply to costs incurred in the 2020 income tax year and in future years, even if the land in question was first held before that date.

Previously, there were some compliance and administrative difficulties associated with the need to rely on a taxpayer's assertion about their intentions as to whether or not they are holding vacant land genuinely to derive assessable income. There is an exemption if a taxpayer is 'carrying on a business'. This includes a business carried on by either the taxpayer (ie the owner of the land) or by a specified related entity, or is leased at arm's length for use in *any* business. The problem arose in this taxpayer election being unable to be tested.

Where holding costs were incurred on or before 30 June 2019, these can be claimed in relation to holding vacant land (eg interest on borrowings to acquire the land, tax, rates, etc) if the land is held for the purpose of:

- gaining or producing assessable income (eg rental income); or
- carrying on a business to gain or produce assessable income.

Holding costs incurred before vacant land actually produces assessable income may be deductible, such as during the initial planning and construction phase of a rental property or business premises. This would broadly be the case where there is no room for doubt that the property proposed to be constructed is to be used for producing assessable income and the nexus with income is not remote. Interest incurred prior to income being earned was generally deductible if all of the following applied:

- the expense is incurred to gain or produce the income, such as rent
- the owner of the land's activities are being undertaken to achieve that purpose
- the expense is not a preliminary expense incurred (like legal fees, council fees or planning fees) and hence a prelude to the future income-earning activity
- the period of expenses being incurred prior to any assessable income being earned must not be so long that the necessary connection between the expenses incurred and the assessable income is lost.

## Holding costs incurred after 30 June 2019

The above rules (pre-2019) relied on a landholder's assertions about why they held 'vacant land'. In effect, the ATO did not feel confident about these taxpayers' assertions and wanted to remove the discretions. It felt that some taxpayers were taking advantage of this by claiming holding costs for land that they did not genuinely hold for income purposes. For example, land may have been stated to be held to build a rental property, but later used to build a sole and principal residence. The changes were made to overcome this issue by denying or limiting deductions that may be claimed by certain taxpayers for their costs relating to holding 'vacant land' unless one of the exceptions applies. Hence, this stated intention is no longer relevant in determining the deductibility of holding costs incurred on vacant land.

The new rules do not apply to a taxpayer that is:

- a company, a superannuation fund other than a self-managed superannuation fund (SMSF), a public unit trust or a managed investment trust; or
- a unit trust or partnership of which all the members are entities of the above type.

These entities can continue to claim deductions for vacant land holding costs in accordance with the usual requirements for deductibility. The ATO considers these entities to have a low risk of incorrectly claiming deductions for vacant land, as they are either not controlled by individuals, do not receive tax concessions that flow to individuals, or both.

## Denied deductions may be added to cost base

Any costs that are not deductible under the new 2019 rules cannot be carried forward and deducted in later years. Instead, they are included in the property's cost base for CGT purposes. This can create a cash flow problem, as the costs will be incurred before the asset is sold and, while it will increase the cost base of the land and hence reduce the CGT payable, this event will only occur when the land is sold. Of course, if the gain is reduced by the 50 per cent CGT discount, then the full benefit of these holding costs will be lost.

## What is the definition of 'vacant land'?

One of the options to avoid losing the deduction for holding costs is to construct a dwelling of some type. The definition of a vacant land is stated as 'there is no substantial and permanent structure in use or available for use on the land having a purpose that is independent of, and not incidental to, the purpose of any other structure or proposed structure'.

A structure includes a building or other edifice that is built or constructed on the land:

- **Substantial and permanent structure.** To be substantial, a building or other structure must be 'significant in size, value or some other criteria of importance' in the context of the relevant property. Unfortunately, there is no guidance on what this means except in the negative. For example, a structure is not substantial if it only has value as an *adjunct* to another structure. For example, a residential garage would be an adjunct to any future residential property to be constructed.
- **In use or available for use.** This term will be interpreted broadly. As long as a substantial and permanent structure is capable of being used (eg residential or commercial premises are habitable and otherwise able to be occupied), it will generally be treated as being in use or available for use.
- **An independent (and not incidental) purpose to the purpose of any other structure or proposed structure on the land.** Alternatively, a woolshed for shearing and baling wool and a grain silo would all usually have an independent purpose (rather than being incidental to

some other structure) as they operate separately from, and independent of, any other structure on the land.

To be permanent, a structure must be fixed and enduring (and not built for a temporary purpose), even if it is not expected to remain standing forever.

## Vacant land purchased for future rental property

If you purchased a block of land to build a rental property, until this dwelling is built, you cannot deduct any holding costs incurred from 1 July 2019. This would also apply if the land was rented, say, to a builder for storage of building materials or agistment, unless one of the exceptions noted below applied.

## Construction of a residential rental property

To illustrate the timing issues (post 1 July 2019 changes), assume you intended to construct a residential rental property and you purchased a vacant block of land in December 2018. You enter into a building contract and start building in August 2019. The property is finished in March 2020. You engage a real estate agent and list the property for rent on 1 July 2020.

- **For the 2019 tax year,** you can claim deductions for all holding costs, even though no rental income has been received for the 2019 income year.
- **For the 2020 tax year,** due to the changes that apply from 1 July 2019, no holding costs can be claimed until the

property is available for rent. This will be when you give it to the agent to find a tenant. Of course, the property must have an occupation certificate and be capable of being occupied. You will need to add these costs to the cost base of the property.

## Construction of a commercial rental property

Where the rental property being constructed is a commercial rental property, deductions for holding costs will be denied until an eligible substantial and permanent structure is 'in use or available for use' on the land. Commercial rental properties are not subject to the legislative extension of 'vacant land'. The October 2019 changes to vacant land only apply to newly constructed or substantially renovated residential rental properties (which require the property to be constructed, legally able to be occupied, and either rented or available for rent).

As to when a property is 'in use or available for use', this is less onerous than the additional requirements that apply for constructed (or substantially renovated) residential premises.

## Holding costs incurred during repair/ renovation period

Assume you purchased a pre-existing residential rental property on 1 July 2019 and rented it to tenants immediately following its purchase. On 30 June 2024, the tenants vacate the property, and you decide to undertake some minor repairs and renovations by painting the internal rooms and updating the kitchen benchtops and cupboards. The renovations are classified as being 'substantially renovated' during your ownership period. Of course, you cannot rent the property until the renovations are completed and hence it is vacant. You finish the renovations on 1 November 2024 and your agent lists it for rent. The question is, can you claim holding cost deductions during the repair and renovation period? The answer is yes, as there is an eligible substantial and permanent structure on the land 'in use or available for use' during this period. The exclusions in the 2019 changes will have no application.

## The 'primary producer' exception

An exception has been introduced to exempt primary producers from the current (1 July 2019) 'vacant land' non-deductibility rules. If all of the following apply, primary producers will be exempted from the vacant land provisions that apply from 1 July 2019 and hence able to claim the holding costs relating to vacant land:

- The land is under lease, hire or licence to another entity.
- The taxpayer or a specified related entity (as discussed earlier) is carrying on a primary production business.
- The land does not contain residential premises.
- Residential premises are not being constructed on the land.

The criteria is very restrictive and onerous to gain the exception. Frankly, there would be very few situations where all of the above conditions can be met. However, if they can be met, the holding costs are allowed to be claimed. This is especially true if the land is used to produce income. If they can't be met, the income would be assessable and the expenses not claimable, which seems crazy but true.

## Examples of the traps in the vacant land rules

### Example 1

A mother and father (or a specified related entity) own vacant farm land. They are retired and so not (directly or indirectly) engaged in any primary production activities. The land contains no residential premises, and no such premises are being constructed on the land. The land is leased to their adult son, at below market rate, for use in his primary production business.

The parents will be denied expenses, which will include their holding costs relating to the land, but will need to declare the rent received as income, for the following reasons:

- Neither the 'carrying on a business' exception nor the 'primary producer' exception apply. This is because the son is not a specified related entity for the purposes of those exceptions (as he is at least 18 years old), and neither of the parents (or a specified related entity) are primary producers.
- The extended 'carrying on (any) business' exception also does not apply because the property is leased to the son for below market value. (Hint: If you satisfied the 'carrying on a business' requirement then the parents may be wise to rent the land to their son at market value and hence satisfy this requirement.)

### Example 2

A taxpayer owns a few acres of vacant land that they lease to an unrelated party for market rent. Neither the taxpayer nor any specified related entities carry on a primary production business. The lessee is not carrying on a business and wishes to use the land for private purposes (eg to agist a few horses they keep because they enjoy horse riding, or for their family's BMX bike riding).

The landholder will be denied deductions for their holding costs, as the land is leased to an entity that is not carrying on a business. The onus is on the landholder to know that the lessee is not carrying on a business. Furthermore, the 'primary producer' exception does not assist as the landholder (or a specified related entity) is not currently carrying on a primary production business. Despite this, the landholder is fully assessable on the rent they receive.

### Example 3

A primary producer decides to build a residential property on a part of their farm that is unsuitable for farming purposes. There are currently no structures on the land. The residential property will be used to derive rental income. All holding costs will be denied for the portion of the land used to build the residential premises (ie the part that is not used or available for use in carrying on a business) until all of the below are satisfied:

- construction of the residential property is complete
- approval to occupy the property is granted
- the property is genuinely available for rent.

The provisions relating to vacant land are complicated. When you are considering constructing a rental property, you need to be aware that, from 2020 onwards, all holding costs will be added to the cost base and hence not deductible. If possible, with the knowledge of how this area works, you should try as hard as possible to limit these non-deductible expenses. You may try to time the demolition of any existing structures or bring forward the available for-rent period. This will limit the time period that such expenses will be quarantined and added to the cost base of the property. Otherwise, the effect on your cash flow by not getting a tax deduction will be severely affected.

29

# Tax tip 7 – salary and wages trap: how to break free

As an employee, claiming tax deductions is difficult and requires care. This is one area the ATO focuses on. Unfortunately, over half the money the ATO collects is from salary and wage earners ($233 billion in 2021 against total collections of $451 billion [ATO Annual Report 2021, p 67]). This is why it is so important to think ahead and plan. As a salary and wage earner, you are caught in a 'work for a living' trap. The only way to get out of this trap is to accumulate assets that will give you passive income.

Earlier in this book I covered the initial deposit syndrome, and how to break free from the burden of selling your time for income and move to a passive income stream. I also listed ten tips to break the poverty trap. It is not easy and takes discipline to accumulate sufficient savings to buy your first house, obtain a massive tax refund and then buy your second property, then third home, and so on. This is where you can stand out from the masses, those that spend their surplus income on 'quick fix' enjoyment and then retire on a pension that will keep them in poverty.

Saving hard, using a tax refund, using a small windfall gain or using a loan from your parents are the leg-up that is needed to start the process. It is what will set you apart from the average person.

A typical example is one reported in the press. It is the story of Victor Kumar, a medical worker who migrated to Australia from Fiji with his wife, with less than $5000 to their names. He received a workplace injury payout of $8000. He used it to purchase a unit for $70,000 in Darwin. They set their sights on property investment as a vehicle to a more financially secure future. They followed the strategy outlined in this book.

'It was a hard slog in the initial stages, we sacrificed a lot, we started our family late, we didn't have much of a social life in the early stages,' he said. The couple now own more than 100 rental properties, with an additional 30 being built (G Cann, 'Data reveals small number of property investors control big chunk of Australian rentals', *ABC*, 17 October 2024).

It is not easy, but it is the only way to start the process to save as much as possible to enable that first purchase. This will be a life-changing event that you must do to get onto the first rung of the wealth creation ladder. I will repeat my earlier example below of what the first year of ownership of your first property could look like. In this example you can see that the ATO subsidises your annual costs to the tune of $37,600. Your cash loss is only $7400 per annum.

**Figure 38 Tax effect on a single property**

| | |
|---|---|
| Purchase price | 1,000,000 |
| | |
| Rent income | 45,000 |
| Expenses | |
| Depreciation | 35,000 |
| Rates and taxes | 15,000 |

| | |
|---|---|
| Interest on loan | 60,000 |
| Repairs | 15,000 |
| Total expenses | 125,000 |

| | |
|---|---|
| Net loss | –80,000 |
| Tax benefit or refund at 47% | 37,600 |
| After-tax loss | –42,400 |
| Add back depreciation (non-cash item) | 35,000 |
| Net cash loss | –7,400 |

This is the break-free (of working for a living) strategy you need to embark on. Many Australians are following this exact strategy.

Information obtained by the ABC from ATO (using the Freedom of Information laws) reports that at least 2500 investors in Australia own or part-own ten or more rental properties. These investors control more than 33,200 rentals, according to CoreLogic data supplied to the ABC. There are 172 investors with interests in 20 or more properties. These investors have interests in 4395 rentals between them.

This does not include rental properties held in companies or trusts, or properties that are vacant. It may include commercial properties, if they are in an individual's names. It should be noted that taxpayers with large portfolios do have a lot of debt associated with that portfolio. Of course, they are using the system to grow their wealth and banks to help them do that. It is also the case that those who own less than 20 properties show a taxable profit, while those who own more than 20 show a loss. I would suspect that those owning more than 20 are building their portfolio. Then, when built and it is time to retire, they sell down assets, pay off debt and live on the passive income being generated by their massive rental portfolio.

Many people on fixed incomes such as nurses, police officers and medical workers have educated themselves that the only way to get ahead is to use the tax system to help them build a massive property portfolio.

While the information obtained from the ATO statistics indicated 2500 individual investors own ten or more properties, my view is that this is extremely conservative. I know from my experience that often different entities are used, and so it is more likely ten times this number. In many cases, we recommend other entities and various other structures, such as unit trusts or your super fund. Hence, not all properties are held in a taxpayer's personal name, particularly where a property will be positively geared.

If you want to get out of the tax trap, you need to start. I know it is not easy making that first acquisition, but it is the only way. Negative gearing, being clever and following the tips outlined in this book is the only way. Spend time investing in your future, spend time looking for opportunities, spend time investigating and planning. The first step is what will set you apart from those that say it is all too hard. Be one of the many Australians that have a smile on their face because they know that their future is secure. If tomorrow they lose their job, it won't matter: they now control their finances.

30

# Tax tip 8 – share portfolios as a business

In this section, I have covered many of the tax tips associated with buying and selling property. But property is not the only asset class. I have previously discussed owning shares. In this chapter, I want to be specific about shares and share portfolios. There are some specific rules that apply to shares that you need to be aware of. As each situation can vary dramatically, you should always seek professional advice. Some of these rules apply to all asset classes, some do not (and, of course, legislation and case law can change the rules):

- Are you carrying on a business as a share trader or are you a share investor?
- If you have borrowed money – hence gearing your portfolio – when can you claim the interest incurred?
- Are you able to use the 50 per cent CGT exemption, even though you have held a share for more than 12 months?
- Will you lose the franking credits?
- What is the Wash Rule and how does it affect my ability to offset capital gains to capital losses?

- How can the ability to offset my share-trading losses to my salary be denied under Division 35 of the Tax Act?

The tax treatment of shares depends on whether you're considered to be holding shares as an investor or carrying on a business as a share trader.

In tax (and accounting), there are two terms: capital account or revenue account. This is covered in the property section and the same rules apply. An investor incurs expenses that are on capital, whereas a trader incurs expenses on revenue account. This affects whether certain costs are accumulated and claimed as part of the cost base (and hence reduce the CGT payable when the asset is sold) or are deducted immediately if you are carrying on a business. If you are a share trader, interest, gains and losses are all taxable/deductible in a year, regardless of whether you have actually sold the shares. A little like trading stock.

This is a complicated area, so it's worth considering how the rules apply to you; in other words, how the transactions will give you the best tax outcome based on the manner in which you conduct your share-trading activities.

## What is a share investor?

To be classified as a share investor (as distinct from carrying on the business of share trading), the intention must be that the shares are purchased and held for the purpose of earning income from dividends and similar receipts. The tax effect is that:

- the cost of the purchase of shares is not an allowable deduction against current year income but is a capital cost (and CGT discount if you qualify) and subject to tax when sold

- receipts from the sale of shares are not assessable income, but any capital gain on the shares is subject to CGT
- a net capital loss from the sale of shares can't be offset against (ordinary) income from other sources but can be offset against another capital gain or carried forward to offset against future capital gains
- the transaction costs of buying or selling shares is not an allowable deduction against income, it forms part of the cost base of the shares and is taken into account in determining the amount of any capital gain
- dividends and other similar receipts from the shares are included in assessable income
- costs (such as interest on borrowed money) incurred in earning dividend income are an allowable deduction against current year income.

## Share trading as a business

A person is deemed to be a share trader if they carry out their business for the purpose of earning income from buying and selling shares. Hence, the tax position for a share trader is that:

- receipts from the sale of shares constitute assessable income
- shares purchased are regarded as trading stock
- costs incurred in buying or selling shares, including the cost of the shares, are an allowable deduction in the year in which they are incurred

- shares held on 30 June are treated as closing stock and valued in accordance with the trading stock rules. These rules are very flexible and allow shares to be taken up at the lower of cost or net realisable value (market value). A determination can be made for every share held based on any or either of the above closing stock rules. Closing stock in one year is opening stock in the following year
- dividends and other similar receipts are included in assessable income
- costs (such as interest on borrowed money) incurred in earning income are an allowable deduction against current year income.

## How do you decide whether you're carrying on a business of share trading or simply holding shares for investment purposes?

The rules on whether or not you're carrying on a business of share trading are the same rules that apply to any other undertaking for tax purposes. In accordance with the definition contained in Section 41 of the *New Tax System (Australian Business Number) Act 1999* and clarified within Taxation Ruling TR 2019/1, a 'business' includes 'any profession, trade, employment, vocation or calling, but does not include occupation as an employee'. The question of whether a person is a share trader or a long-term share investor has been determined by case law. Everyone's situation can be different, so sometimes it can be difficult to be certain which way the ATO will treat your activities. You can seek a private ruling to clarify this. Often, taxpayers challenge the ATO and the court position, and hence many rulings and determinations have been made on this point alone. These rulings are centred around the following four areas, which are explained in further detail. It is a very important distinction, and care must be taken should you choose to adopt a particular path (as a share trader or as a share investor):

1. The nature of the activities, particularly whether they have the purpose of profit making.
2. The repetition, volume and regularity of the activities, and the similarity to other businesses in your industry.
3. Organisation in a business-like way, including keeping accounts and records of trading stock, business premises, licences or qualifications, a registered business name and an Australian business number.
4. The amount of capital invested.

### Nature of activity and purpose of profit making

We all enter into a business transaction to make a profit. However, sometimes the circumstances work against us, and this is not the case. We often see situations where a loss has been made and the person now seeks to claim those losses as trading losses, especially if they want to offset these losses against other income like their salary. If they made a gain, they may try to say they are an investor and, hence, will not need to declare the gains until the shares are sold. We therefore have two possible intentions when shares are purchased. The first could be to make a profit on the purchase and then sale of those shares. The second could be just to earn a great dividend and perhaps a future capital gain. Sometimes, when shares are purchased, these intentions can be mixed, as you may want both. Making a short-term profit on some share sales, does not, on its own, indicate a business is being carried on, sufficient to satisfy the ATO criteria. Shares held for investment and for trading both have the same characteristics yet a totally different tax outcome. A person may buy shares to sell at a profit, or they may buy shares to hold for dividend reasons. Therefore, not only is the intention important but also the facts surrounding the manner in which the taxpayer conducts their activities. This may include preparing a detailed business plan that may cover the following:

- Reviewing each investment or potential investment made.
- An overview of the share market and where the market might be heading.
- Research conducted on when the activities will start making profits and how much profit you expect to earn.
- A set of assumptions may be created that will set the basis on when to buy or sell a particular share. For example when a share increase or decreases above or below a certain amount. These assumptions may also set parameters and rules for 'stop loss' points – when to realise a profit and when to hold.

### Repetition, volume and regularity

If you are carrying on a business, generally you would expect that there are a high number of transactions occurring. The higher the number of buys and sells, the more likely it is that you are carrying on a share-trading business. As a trader, it would be expected that these transactions would be regular, constant and involve a reasonable volume.

### Acting in a business-like way and keeping records

If you are running a business, it could be expected that you are conducting your business in a business-like manner. This will include studying company prospectuses, attending share-trading courses and attending annual general meetings. As a business owner it would also be expected that you maintain proper books of account, which may also include using appropriate share-trading software.

### Amount of capital invested

This is not a crucial factor but it does assist in determining if you are carrying on a business. For example, if you purchased one share, it would be hard to say you are carrying on a share-trading business. However, case law has helped decide this difficult criteria.

Let me illustrate the above with two examples from our client base.

#### Case study 1: A share investor

Mrs G has been buying shares for 30 years. She rarely sells any shares and has amassed a portfolio of some 20 stocks that have a cost base of around $2 million and a market value of $6 million. She lives off the dividends, which are now around $300,000 per year. She is treated as a share investor (not a trader). She only pays tax on shares when they are sold and is able to avail herself of any capital gains tax discounts on the sale.

#### Case study 2: A share trader

Mr N logs on every day to the share market. His computer has three screens, and he actively watches all movements. In a day, he might buy and sell the same stock, he might open positions with CFD (contracts for difference) to short sell or buy. At the end of the year, all shares held are treated as closing stock. Gains or losses during the year will be taxable or deductible. All unrealised gains will be taxable, and all unrealised losses will be deductible. The cost of running his office and all costs associated with his business are deductible. He is active in the mining sector. In doing his research, he sometimes visits those mines. All of these costs will also be deductible.

In summary, the advantages of carrying on a business as a share trader are the following:

- Share traders can offset any trading losses incurred over the financial year against other assessable income (subject to the rules contained in Division 35 of the Tax Act which may serve to quarantine these losses if one of the requirements in this section are not met).
- Costs incurred in buying or selling shares are an allowable deduction in the year in which they are incurred.
- All costs associated with running the business will be deductible.

The bad news is that they can't take advantage of the 50 per cent capital gains discount on shares held for more than 12 months.

The best way of looking at it is that share traders buy and sell shares for profit, whereas share investors buy shares to hold as an investment. In the same vein as other businesses, any profits made by the share trader are regarded as assessable income, and all costs incurred in running the business are deductible.

## Gearing and loans associated with buying shares

While the determination on whether you are a share investor or carrying on the business of share investment affects many deductions, it does not affect claiming a tax deduction for interest paid to purchase shares. They must be shares that will or are likely to pay a dividend. This is because both a share investor and a share-trading business will incur these costs. The tax tip on this is that by using gearing, you are able to both multiply gains but also multiply losses. Gearing has tax advantages and you can also use the prepayment rules to maximise your tax deductions. As a rule, it is usually prudent to only gear around 30 per cent of any share portfolio due to the inherent volatility of shares. Hence, with gearing, $70,000 cash and a $30,000 bank loan allows $100,000 to be invested into the share market. The same rules apply to rental property.

This will be a personal decision. I have seen many clients gear 100 per cent on blue chip shares and come out in front. I have seen others lose substantial sums. Be careful and seek advice. Share trading is not for the faint hearted. We had one client who boasted about his share-trading skills. He lost $7 million over a ten-year period.

## Limiting rules – to be able to receive a franking credit refund

Your entitlement to a franking credit may be affected by the holding period rule, the related payments rule or the dividend washing integrity rule. The general effect of the holding period rule and the related payments rule is that even if a dividend is accompanied by a dividend statement advising that there is a franking credit attached to the dividend, you are not entitled to claim the franking credit.

The entitlement to a franking credit can also be affected if you enter into a scheme with the dominant purpose of obtaining franking credits (referred to as franking credit trading).

### Holding period rule

The holding period rule requires you to continuously hold shares 'at risk' for at least 45 days (90 days for certain preference shares) to be eligible for the franking credit. However, under the small shareholder exemption, this rule does not apply if your total franking credit entitlement is below $5000. This is roughly equivalent to receiving a fully franked dividend of:

- $11,666 (for companies that are not base rate entities, with a corporate tax rate of 30 per cent); or
- $13,181 (for companies that are base rate entities, with a corporate tax rate of 27.5 per cent).

The holding period does not include the day of acquisition or disposal of the shares. The financial risk of owning shares may be reduced through arrangements such as hedges, options and futures. In this case the holding period is 90 days, instead of 45 days.

If you acquire shares, or an interest in shares, and you have not already satisfied the holding period rule before the day on which the shares become ex-dividend, the holding period rule commences on the day after the day on which you acquired the shares or interest. The shares become ex-dividend on the day after the last day on which acquisition of the shares will entitle you to receive the dividend. You must then hold the shares or interest (at risk) for 45 days (90 days for certain preference shares), excluding the day of disposal. For each of these days, you must have 30 per cent or more of the ordinary financial risks of loss and opportunities for gain from owning the shares or interest.

You have to satisfy the holding period rule once only for each purchase of shares. You are then entitled to the franking credits attached to those shares, unless the related payments rule applies.

### The wash rule – affecting profits and losses on sale of shares

It is common if you have made a substantial gain on the sale of shares, and you are also holding shares that have decreased in value, to consider selling them to offset the gains made on other shares. However, the tax office is aware of this strategy, and while it is difficult to prove, you need to be aware that it exists. If, for instance, you sold some loss-making shares on 30 June and bought them back on 1 July, that would clearly show intention. The tax office has issued tax ruling TR 2008/1, also known as *Income tax: application of Part 4A of the Income Tax Assessment Act 1936*, to 'wash sale' arrangements. The effect will be to deny the loss being claimed as an offset against the capital gain.

Be mindful that this rule exists and be careful with how any such transaction is conducted.

The above rules are complicated, so you need to be careful that you comply with them. This will ensure any gains, franking credits or any issues associated with building wealth through the acquisition of shares are complied with. Most are reasonably easy to comply with if you are aware that they exist and take measures to ensure you do not inadvertently do something to cause the loss of the concession. If you are unsure, seek professional help.

## Related payments rule

If you pass on the benefit of a franking credit to someone else, this could be treated as a related payment. This may occur in a trust or partnership where the dividend and hence franking credit passes to someone else. If this rule is not satisfied the franking credit will be lost, even though you may have satisfied the holding period rule. This rule applies to each parcel of shares held, each dividend payment and each distribution you make.

## Division 35 – non-commercial losses

Division 35 is a cruel division that was introduced due to many people operating a business that could only be called a hobby, as it never had any chance of ever making a profit. The effect is to not allow an individual who conducts a business and loses money on that business to offset those losses to their other income (such as a salary). This provision does not apply to rental property losses, only to business losses. A share trader that is operating as a business can be caught by this Division.

The ruling sets out four tests, only one of which you need to pass in order to not be caught under this Division.

1. **Assessable Income Test:** The business activity has an assessable income (not profit) of at least $20,000.
2. **Profits Test:** The business has made a tax profit in three out of the past five years (including the current year).
3. **Real Property Test:** Real property valued at least $500,000 is used in the business on a continuing basis.
4. **Other Assets Test:** Other assets (such as plant and equipment, trading stock, patents or trademarks; but

excluding real property, cars, motorcycles, etc) valued at least $100,000 are used in the business on a continuing basis.

In 2009, an overarching income requirement was introduced, which set an (other) income threshold of $250,000. This means that you are unable to offset the losses against your other income, regardless of whether or not you passed any of the above four tests. This income test is not just based on your salary but requires the add-back of reportable fringe benefits, rental property losses and a few other unusual items.

You can apply to the Commissioner and seek a private ruling to not have these losses quarantined. I have applied for a few of these and, by following the guidelines, was successful. However, if you fail the income test then your ability to obtain a private ruling is made far more difficult, if not impossible.

The ATO has even issued a ruling number TR 2007/6 to help taxpayers know what the Commissioner will and will not consider. You need to be very careful if any of the above applies. The non commercial loss rules apply to any business venture, not just share trading. This is where planning is so important. If your other income, after addbacks, is below the $250,000 threshold, then you may need to consider how you can meet one of the other tests; for example, by ensuring your turnover through share sales will meet the turnover test. If you cannot meet any of the tests or your other income is above the $250,000 threshold, any losses on share trading will be quarantined and available to be offset against any future share-trading profits.

## Tax tip on Division 35

The biggest issue with Division 35 is the other income test. Basically, if you fail this, by having other income over the $250,000 threshold, the ability to use any tax losses with share trading, or any other business losses for that matter, are severely limited. Yes, you must satisfy one of the other four tests after you satisfy the income test. But that part is usually easy. The problem is that once the losses are quarantined, you must satisfy the tests in the future to ever be able to use these losses. One way to handle this is to investigate if the other income (eg the salary), could be reduced with the balance paid as consulting fees into a company or other entity. It needs to be justified and carefully done as Part IVA can apply. You also need to plan in advance, and act before 30 June. This will allow the losses to be used up to the level retained as salary with any excess balance available to be offset against your tax in future years.

31

# Tax tip 9 – year-end tax-planning tips for investors

The only way to get ahead financially is to invest. That investment may take the form of property or shares, and to a limited extent other financial assets like digital currency or currency trading.

Statistically, over 5 million individuals receive dividend income each year ($93 billion in 2019), while 2.1 million have reported rental income totalling $44 billion. According to the ATO, $20 billion in capital gains were reported by almost 700,000 individuals, while more than 900,000 reported capital losses of $27 billion. Assessable foreign sources of income of almost $6 billion were reported by 730,000 individuals.

Before we consider the year-end tips, it is important to know that Big Brother ATO is watching you. Their data-matching and information exchange capabilities continue to evolve and now cover many capital transactions and investment revenue streams, both in Australia and overseas. You must report all investment income, including any income from overseas, and maintain accurate records. You must correctly calculate capital gains or losses on disposal and ensure you comply with the various rules and concessions available to investors.

## Investment income deductions

If you are to claim a deduction for interest or other expenses, the costs must be directly related to the investment. This is covered earlier, but is worth repeating. It is not the security that is used for a loan that determines its deductibility, it is the use that the funds were put to. For example, if you borrow from the bank and use your rental property as security and use the money to pay off your loan on your home, it will not be deductible. If you use it to buy a second rental property or for renovations on a rental property, it will be deductible. Therefore, you can only claim a deduction for expenses incurred in earning rent, interest, dividends or other investment income. But if the use of the funds is to earn tax-exempt dividends, other exempt income or for private and domestic purposes, you cannot claim this interest.

Following is a checklist of the types of deductions claimable:

- account-keeping fees for an account held for investment purposes
- interest charged on money borrowed to buy property, shares and other related investments from which you derive assessable interest or dividend income
- ongoing management fees or retainers and amounts paid for advice relating to changes in the mix of investment
- a portion of other costs incurred in managing your investments, such as some travel expenses (not on residential properties as an individual), investment journals, subscriptions and borrowing costs.

If you attend an investment seminar, you are only entitled to claim a deduction for the portion of travel expenses relating to any investment income activities, but not to inspect your rental property (a harsh exception).

## Rental income

The ATO continues its focus on checking rental deductions and matching reported income against details from Airbnb and other providers. From the 2021 tax year, a multi-property rental schedule for individuals is required to be lodged with your income tax returns. Hence, you cannot bulk up your deductions. You need to apply them to each property.

As a tax tip, be careful as the ATO has focused on the following:

- deductions for properties where tenants are not paying their full rent or have temporarily stopped paying rent as their income is affected by unemployment or health issues
- assessable receipts of back payments of rent or an amount of insurance for lost rent
- interest deductions on deferred loan repayments for a period due to mortgage stress or bank hardship concessions
- the private use of a rental property by the owner – such as a holiday home when not rented – and adjusting the available tax deductions
- changes to advertising and other fees for short-term rental properties due to no demand for the property.

If, for example, a property is only available for rent 75 per cent of the year, then only 75 per cent of the costs associated with that property will be deductible. The property is not available for rent for the other 25 per cent of the year.

## Ten most common mistakes that rental owners make

### 1 Apportioning expenses and income for co-owned properties

If you own a rental property with someone else, you must declare rental income and claim expenses according to your legal ownership of the property. As joint tenants, your legal interest will be an equal split, and as tenants in common, you may have different ownership interests. The ATO, in accordance with tax rulings, assumes a 50 per cent split when there is no documentation or legal ownership structure that defines a different percentage.

### 2 Making sure your property is genuinely available for rent

Your property must be genuinely available for rent to claim a tax deduction. This means:

- you must be able to show a clear intention to rent the property
- advertising the property so that someone is likely to rent it and set the rent in line with similar properties in the area
- avoiding unreasonable rental conditions.

Be aware that any related party discounts may limit your tax deduction; for example, if you rent your property at a discount to your parents or children.

### 3 Getting initial repairs and capital improvements right

Ongoing repairs that relate directly to wear and tear or other damage that happened as a result of you renting out the property can be claimed in full in the same year you incurred the expense. For example, repairing the hot water system or part of a damaged roof can be deducted immediately. Initial repairs for damage that existed when the property was purchased, such as replacing broken light fittings and repairing damaged floorboards, are not immediately deductible. Instead, these costs are added to your cost base and used to work out your capital gain or capital loss when you sell the property. Replacing an entire structure, like a roof when only part of it is damaged, or renovating a bathroom is classified as an improvement and not immediately deductible. These are building costs that you can claim at 2.5 per cent each year for 40 years from the date of completion. If you completely replace a damaged item that is detachable from the house and it costs more than $300 (eg replacing the entire hot water system), the cost must be depreciated over a number of years.

### 4 Claiming borrowing expenses

If your borrowing expenses are over $100, the deduction is spread over five years. If they are $100 or less, you can claim the full amount in the same income year you incurred the expense. Borrowing expenses include loan establishment fees, title search fees and costs of preparing and filing mortgage documents.

### 5 Claiming purchase costs

You can't claim any deductions for the costs of buying your property. These include conveyancing fees and stamp duty (for properties outside the ACT). If you sell your property, these costs are then used when working out whether you need to pay capital gains tax.

### 6 Claiming interest on your loan

You can claim interest as a deduction if you take out a loan for your rental property. If you use some of the loan money for personal use, such as buying a boat or going on a holiday, you can't claim the interest on that part of the loan. You can only claim the part of the interest that relates to the rental property.

### 7 Getting construction costs right

You can claim certain building costs, including extensions, alterations and structural improvements, as capital works deductions. As a general rule, you can claim a capital works deduction at 2.5 per cent of the construction cost for 40 years from the date the construction was completed. Where your property was owned by someone else previously and they claimed capital works deductions, ask them to provide you with the details so you can correctly calculate the deduction you're entitled to claim. If you can't obtain those details from the previous owner, you can use the services of a quantity surveyor to prepare what is called a QS report. This report will provide the details you need to claim the correct depreciation write-offs.

### 8 Claiming the right portion of your expenses

If your rental property is rented out to family or friends below market rate, you can only claim a deduction for that period up to the amount of rent you received. You can't claim deductions when your family or friends stay free of charge, or for periods of personal use.

### 9 Keeping the right records

You must have evidence of your income and expenses so you can claim everything you are entitled to. Capital gains tax may apply when you sell your rental property, so keep records over the period you own the property and for five years from the date you sell the property.

### 10 Getting your capital gains right when selling

When you sell your rental property, you may make either a capital gain or a capital loss. Generally, this is the difference between what it costs you to buy and improve the property, and what you receive when you sell it. Your costs must not include amounts already claimed as a deduction against rental income earned from the property, including depreciation and capital works. If you make a capital gain, you will need to include the gain in your tax return for that income year. If you make a capital loss, you can carry the loss forward and deduct it from capital gains in later years.

Owners of properties being rented or which are ready and available for rent can claim immediate deductions for a range of expenses, such as:

- interest on investment loans
- land tax
- council and water rates
- body corporate charges insurance
- repairs and maintenance
- agent's commission
- gardening
- pest control
- leases – preparation, registration and stamp duty
- advertising for tenants.

Depreciation, for me, has always been a big item, as it is a non-cash expenditure. As a landlord, you will be entitled to claim annual deductions for the declining value of depreciable assets, such as stoves, carpets and hot water systems. This includes capital works deductions spread over a number of years for structural improvements, like remodelling a bathroom. To do so, you may need to obtain a depreciation report from a quantity surveyor, a cost that will be more than paid for in depreciation claims.

Deductions for the depreciation of plant and equipment for residential real estate properties are limited to outlays actually incurred on new items by the investor. For example, for properties acquired after 9 May 2017, landlords can no longer depreciate assets already in the property at the time of purchase. However, should they purchase a new – not used or refurbished – asset, they can depreciate that asset.

Plant and equipment forming part of residential investment properties as of 9 May 2017 will continue to give rise to deductions for depreciation until either the investor no longer owns the asset or the asset reaches the end of its effective life.

The ATO, in its wisdom, made changes to deny landlords the travel costs relating to inspecting, maintaining or collecting rent for a residential rental property. To me, that is wrong as these costs are rightly attributable to the earning of rental income. They remain deductible for a commercial property or where a property is owned in a unit trust or company structure.

Ensure interest expense claims are correctly calculated and rental income is correctly apportioned between owners. This ensures claims for costs to repair damage or defects at the time of purchase are depreciated and holiday homes are genuinely available for rent.

## Deductions for vacant land

This area is covered in greater detail earlier in this book, but here is a summary. Changes to legislation to limit deductions claimed for holding vacant land received royal assent on 28 October 2019. These changes apply to costs incurred on or after 1 July 2019, even if the land was held before that date.

Deductions for expenses incurred for holding costs of vacant land can continue to be claimed by corporate tax entities and superannuation funds other than self-managed superannuation funds, as well as managed investment trusts, public unit trusts and unit trusts or partnerships where all the members are the previous entity types.

There are some entities and circumstances where deductions for vacant land can still be claimed. For example, where the entity holding the land is a company, you use the land in carrying on a business or exceptional circumstances apply. Expenses of holding land remain deductible if they are incurred in carrying on a business, such as farming, or gaining or producing assessable income. Refer to Chapter 28 for a full explanation on the deductions available for vacant land.

## Residential property and non-residents

A change in law on 12 December 2019 removed the main residence exemption for all property owned by non-residents. The start date is 1 July 2020. The effect is that for a non-resident that sells their property on or before 30 June 2020, they will be able to qualify for the exemption from CGT for their main residence. If they sell it after 30 June 2020 they will not qualify for this exemption unless they satisfy the life events test. The life events test requires that they are a foreign resident for a continuous period of six years or less and during that time either they, their spouse or dependants under 18 had a terminal medical condition, their spouse or their child under 18 died, or the sale of their property was because of a formal agreement after a breakdown of their marriage or relationship.

For properties held before 7.30 pm (AEST) on 9 May 2017, the CGT main residence exemption will only be able to be claimed for disposals that happened up until 30 June 2020, provided the taxpayer satisfies the other existing requirements for the exemption.

The definition of your residency status for tax purposes is not your migration status or citizenship, nor is it related to this. You are a resident for tax purposes once you have earned income in Australia. Therefore, you must lodge a tax return, regardless of whether you're a resident or non-resident in your migration status or a resident or non-resident for tax purposes. This is an extremely confusing area and subject to many tax rulings and court cases.

## Tax clearance certificate

From 1 January 2025, it is mandatory for all persons who sell a property to obtain a tax clearance certificate. The clearance certificate must be given to the buyer before settlement. Previously for residents of Australia, this only applied if a property sale was over $750,000. The withholding rate was previously 12.5 per cent. It now applies to all property sales and the withholding rate is 15 per cent.

If a person sells a property in Australia and is a non-resident, the buyer must deduct withholding tax at 15 per cent of the sale price and remit this to the ATO. The seller must then lodge an income tax return and declare the taxable profit. If, for example, the seller has a loss on the sale, then the full withholding tax is refunded. If the seller has a profit, the difference between the tax withheld and the tax payable as a non-resident on the profit will be either payable or refundable (whichever is the case).

If the seller does not obtain this clearance certificate, withholding tax must be withheld by the buyer and remitted to the Australian Tax Office on settlement. Clearance certificates can take up to 28 days, although in my experience they only take about a week. But be careful you do not get caught on this one. The tax withheld is credited against your tax account with the ATO and offset against any taxes payable, or will be refunded if no tax is payable when you lodge your income tax return. The issue is that this balancing up can only occur when you lodge your income tax return. If you sold a property in July 2025 and do not have a tax clearance certificate, the 15 per cent deducted will not be refunded until you lodge your 2026 income tax return, which at the earliest would be in July 2026. Also, you will need to have a tax file number and be in the ATO's system to enable the credit to be placed against your tax account with the ATO. I can foresee massive issues with this, especially if previously you did not lodge income tax returns because your income did not require it, you no longer have a tax file number or you are an overseas resident.

## Cryptocurrencies and crowdfunding

The ATO is now matching transaction data obtained from digital exchanges, so it is more important than ever to ensure cryptocurrency gains and losses are correctly reported. If you are currently, or have been, involved in acquiring or selling cryptocurrencies in the past, you need to be aware of the income tax consequences. These vary depending on the nature of your circumstances.

All cryptocurrency traders must keep appropriate records for income tax purposes. If you have dealt with a foreign exchange and/or cryptocurrency, there may also be taxation consequences for your transactions in the foreign country.

Be aware that when you sell one digital asset and buy another, you have created a taxable transaction. Assuming you are an investor (not a trader), you will have created a capital gain based on the sale value, less the cost base of that crypto asset. An investor will get a 50 per cent CGT discount, providing the asset is held for more than 12 months. A trader will not.

Now comes the difficult part, which I have seen happen. Suppose you have sold and made $10 million in capital or trading gains before 30 June. You have invested those sales back into more crypto assets. Then in July, those assets have a major issue and become worthless. You now have a tax bill on a gain of $10 million, with no assets to sell to cover this tax. It would be wise if, before 30 June, you have made a gain, to set aside some of this money to cover the likely tax payable.

The tax consequences of crowdfunding vary, depending on the nature of the arrangement and your role: investor as in share investor, or crypto trader, similar to a share trader; a promoter; or an intermediary earning commission or margin income.

With crypto and crowdfunding, the tax laws apply to the investment and financial activity in the usual manner that applies to any person carrying on a business (review the section on share trading for an outline of this). For example, buying goods and services, shares or lending money is the same as investments and financial activity conducted under crowdfunding and crypto buying and selling.

If you are involved in cryptocurrencies or crowdfunding, you should ensure that you obtain professional advice. The ATO has issued a tax ruling on the treatment of both. It has also confirmed that it is presently data matching all transactions from various exchanges. I have even seen audits as a result of this data matching. I have also seen details of crypto transactions appear on taxpayer prefill reports, similar to property and share sale transactions.

## Rollover relief provisions

It is interesting how people can get this wrong. For example, many people think that if you sell a rental property, the capital gain can be rolled over into the new property that you purchase. My gym instructor said he was told if he sold a rental property and put the money into his super fund, that would surely be a rollover. I needed to tell him that this advice was wrong. Firstly, a sale to a related entity, even though it was his super fund, was still a sale and would generate a capital gain. Secondly, there are various limits on transfers to his superannuation that may also preclude such a transfer of funds.

The idea of a rollover is to either create an exemption or to roll the gain into another place or at some future time. The effect is to defer or disregard the capital gain or capital loss.

As stated, rollover relief does not apply to a capital gain you make when you:

- sell an asset and put the proceeds into a superannuation fund
- use the proceeds to purchase an identical or similar asset
- transfer an asset into a superannuation fund.

To repeat, if you sell a rental property and put the proceeds into a superannuation fund or use the proceeds to purchase another rental property, rollover relief is not available. The exemption to this that allows a rollover is when the asset is used in a business (your business) that satisfies either the small business retirement exemption or the active asset test.

Rollover concessions were introduced by the government to provide an exemption when a small business owner purchases a replacement asset or seeks to use the various retirement exemptions to roll the gain either into a new business (within two years) or roll the gain from the sale of a business into their super fund. This later relief also applies to assets used in the business, such as a capital gain on the sale of business premises. As an important tax tip, to qualify, an entity or person making the gain must roll the gain into a super fund. For example, I had a client that operated a rental business. His company sold the rent roll and made a capital gain of about $400,000. The company had two years to either find a new replacement business or roll the gain into his super fund. He chose to take the money out of the company and put it on deposit (as the interest rate was higher in his personal name). Then, before the two years expired, he put the money from his personal account into his super fund. He therefore failed to meet rollover relief criteria. He said his previous accountant advised him that this was okay. Had his company paid the money into his super fund, he would have qualified. He faced a big tax bill on this gain.

Rollover relief can also apply to a share in a company or interest in a trust. The company or trust must meet the active asset test. The market value of the active assets and certain financial instruments of the company or trust must be 80 per cent or more of the total market value of all the assets of the company or trust. Companies that have more than 80 per cent of their assets in, say, passive assets do not meet these criteria. This rollover relief applies when, for example, a company takes over another company and the consideration is paid as shares in the new company (script for script). You are allowed to keep the original cost base as the cost base of the new company shares. Hence, you do not realise a capital gain that is taxable, even though now you have swapped your old shares for shares in the takeover company.

Rollovers basically fall into broad two categories:

1. Same-asset rollovers – shares for shares, unit in trusts for units in trust.
2. Replacement asset rollovers, such as in a business when you sell one machine and buy another, or a property is converted to strata title.

## Tax tips

With this knowledge in place, you can now consider how to legally use the system to your advantage. Think and plan in advance to use the law to your advantage. Don't, for example, miss out on the rollover relief because you get greedy with earning extra interest.

Under tax law, you are taxed on any profits you make in a financial year. This means profits realised, not unrealised (depending on your circumstances and the manner in which the tax rulings apply to you), in the year ending 30 June. If you reinvest that profit into further investments, it does not always reduce your tax payable. There are some rollover provisions as noted earlier, but you may not meet these and they only apply to certain transactions.

A point I want to repeat is one of tax risk. For example, let's say that for the year ended 30 June 2025, you have made $2 million profit on Bitcoin and reinvested that back into, say, Ethereum coins.

Let's also say that on 1 July, those Ethereum coins drop in value to zero, so you have a real cash flow problem. Now, you have tax payable on $2 million but no way of paying that tax, as the money has been lost in a subsequent tax year. I therefore recommend all investors cash out sufficient funds to meet their tax liabilities. The ATO is yet to accept digital currency in payment of a tax bill.

This example, while extreme, applies to all gains. If you made a $500,000 gain on the sale of a rental property and used all of the proceeds to buy a new house or another rental property, you would not have the funds available to pay the tax on the realised gain on the first property. Remember to keep cash flow in mind when it comes to all gains you make in a financial year.

## Capital gains tax planning

These examples indicate that careful planning is needed in the timing of the disposal of an asset that may result in a capital gain. It is important to recognise that the CGT event is triggered on either the contract date or when the contract becomes unconditional (if subject to, say, a finance clause or some other condition), rather than on settlement of the purchase.

This is particularly important where the contract date and settlement of the contract straddle year-end. In these circumstances, it may be preferable, from a cash flow perspective, to defer the CGT event date of the CGT asset to the subsequent year when other relief may be available, such as a capital loss on another asset.

To obtain the 50 per cent CGT discount, be careful to ensure an eligible asset is retained for the 12-month holding period required under the CGT discount rules. These dates are contract date to contract date (not settlement dates). If you were a foreign resident or temporary resident, you lose the capital gain discount on all assets acquired after 8 May 2012 (when the legislation was enacted). If you acquired assets before 8 May 2012, you can still receive a pro rata portion of the 50 per cent discount for the period of ownership up to 8 May 2012. After that date, all gains are taxable in full without the benefit of the 50 per cent CGT discount.

### Foreign investments

If you are an Australian resident with overseas assets, you need to include any capital gains or losses you make on those assets in your tax return. You may have to include income you receive from overseas interests in your tax return. You must declare this income, even if it is held in an overseas bank account. Australia has tax treaties with most countries. This allows you to obtain a tax credit for any overseas withholding taxes deducted from your overseas income.

32

# Tax tip 10 – ATO data matching and review period

It can be very important when you adopt a tax position on something to know how long the ATO can go back and review that position. In other words, how long they have to amend or challenge the tax payable as a consequence thereof. This is sometimes called the 'hold your breath' period.

## Case study 1

One of my clients asked that I prepare the personal income tax returns for his mother and father. In this case, his parents had sold a rental property and needed to calculate (and pay tax on) the capital gain. They said they sold the property in September 2018. I had great difficulty obtaining information as their record-keeping was poor. After some time, I eventually obtained all the details and drafted their tax returns. This was in February 2020. Everything was completed and I was about to lodge their 2019 income tax returns. Then we received a letter from the ATO seeking to amend their 2018 income tax returns. The letter stated that they had sold a property and had not declared the gain. The ATO had already calculated the capital gain. They knew the cost, the sale price and had even estimated items like stamp duty, legal costs and the agent's commission. When checked, it was the same property that the client thought they had sold in 2019. When I approached the client, they finally obtained from their lawyer the settlement statement. The contract of sale was dated June 2018, the property settled in September 2018. The client did not remember the contract date and did not realise that the capital gains tax event was based on the latter of either the date of the contract or the date that the contract becomes unconditional, if there are conditions that must be met, like a finance clause.

The point is that the ATO knew about the sale. They knew all of the items that made up the capital gain and were able to assess a gain with a reasonable amount of certainty. In this case study, there were a few things missing, but the ATO was about 80 per cent right in the numbers.

The ATO has data-matching systems that provide information that can be cross-checked against any taxation returns you lodge. It is currently in its 17th year of data matching. Every year, the ATO gets better and better at it. The current specific areas of data-matching activities include:

- all banks and financial institutions
- all government agencies, which include Centrelink, Child Support Registrar and Department of Home Affairs
- sharebrokers
- real estate agents for rent received and sales of property
- land titles offices in all states
- credit and debit cards banks and other providers
- specialised payment systems

- online selling (eBay, etc)
- ride-sourcing
- motor vehicle registries for the sale and purchase of all vehicles with a purchase price of over $10,000 (the ATO matches this against your income tax return to see if your lifestyle is at odds with the vehicles you buy)
- cryptocurrency and various online wallets being used
- overseas government agencies
- the Department of Foreign Affairs and Trade, to check your residency and movements in and out of Australia.

If you have a financial transaction, rest assured that the ATO will know about it. My advice is not to hide it. Be proactive and declare it. See a professional and get help on how to minimise the tax payable. But don't simply hide your head in the sand and hope the ATO won't catch up with you. It will. The above even applies to a sale of your sole and principal residence, which is tax free. The ATO will know about the sale, so you need to declare it and nominate that it is tax free because of this exemption. The ATO's computers do not always pick up that a sale is tax free and may issue you a nasty letter. Worse, if you have changed your address a few times and the ATO can't find you, it may, in error, issue a default assessment and start legal proceedings against you. Before you know it, you may have a tax debt and a court-imposed penalty that can be costly in legal fees to fix.

This happened to a client who was prosecuted for failing to lodge several years of outstanding tax returns. Such prosecutions are a criminal offence and show up on your record. The client was unaware of this until he applied for a loan. He approached me and, after some research, I discovered that one of the years claimed as outstanding had been lodged. I advised the ATO, and it set about reversing the conviction. As it had gone that far, this process required a pardon signed by the Governor General. When the client received the pardon, he framed it. To this day, it sits on his wall.

My point is: be aware that the ATO can sometimes go down a path without you realising it.

We are presently seeing the same with cryptocurrency. It takes time to catch up, but 'please explain' letters are starting to come out in respect of 2020 crypto transactions, some two years after the event.

## ATO right of review

After you lodge your income tax return, the law limits how far back the ATO can go to amend your tax return. For most taxpayers with simple affairs, the tax office can go back two years; if your tax affairs are more complex, they can go back four years.

You are also far more open to the historical scrutiny of the ATO if you fail to lodge or knowingly lodge a false tax return. In such cases, there is no limit as to how far the ATO can go back. It is therefore important to actually lodge your income tax returns on time or even early, as the time limit may preclude the ATO from making an amendment. We work with a legal firm in Brisbane that refers to this as the 'hold your breath' period. Remember, even with full disclosure, sometimes the law is not certain on what can be claimed. This is illustrated by the fact that the ATO often has cases it loses. So, interpretation can be key. But if the ATO loses its right to amend due to these time restraints, there can be no amendment.

## Case study 2

I have had the aforementioned situation occur with a new client. The client was a beneficiary of a trust and, as such, needed to declare the income distributed to him by that trust. The trust tax return was lodged through a different accountant. Subsequently, the ATO reviewed the trust and disagreed with the treatment of certain items. However, because all the beneficiaries, except my (new) client, had lodged their income tax returns prior to the expiration of the review period, they could not amend them. However, my (new) client's tax return was lodged within the four-year period of review. The ATO reviewed it and amended his tax return. The result was an extra $260,000 in tax. He fought it but was unsuccessful. He felt he should make a claim against his previous accountant for being slack finalising and then lodging his tax return. He stated all the information had been provided to the accountant who sat on it for over 18 months. Had it been completed and lodged promptly, the ATO would have been outside their review period and unable to amend it. A $260,000 lesson on timeliness (or tardiness).

Every year that the client brings his work to me, he mentions this issue and complains about the cost to him of the previous accountant's tardiness.

It is therefore in your interest to keep your lodgements up to date and lodge on time. It is your responsibility to lodge your income tax return on time. If you have delegated this to someone else and they have not complied with it, it is up to you to ensure compliance. It will be you, the taxpayer, who can be fined for late lodgement. It is also good practice to lodge your returns in a timely manner as you never know when an issue may arise that might come back to haunt you particularly if you are in business.

33

# Education and mindset tips – the why

If you are to embark on a journey of wealth creation, you need to get your mindset right. It is true that education around managing money, simple tax matters and an outline of how money truly works is not something taught in schools or places of higher learning. I certainly never came across any of the things covered in this book at university. This may seem odd, but those who excel in creating massive wealth share this knowledge. However, the general population does not.

Every day, clients pass on information they hear from well-meaning friends that is actually wrong, from people who have never been in business or never created wealth (for themselves). The wealthy do help by passing on tips, but sometimes this is lost in the mainstream of being a worker and having the '9 to 5' mentality that can follow from it.

Also, it is a fact that many so-called financial planners who spruik wealth creation strategies are, in reality, spruiking wealth creation strategies for themselves at your expense, selling on high commission, inflated assets that only harm their clients.

Wealth creation education is lacking in schools, which results in school leavers having no basic money, investment or tax knowledge.

If they are lucky, they may have their parents as role models. If not, they will be sadly unprepared to enter the work force, save for their own future retirement or have any basic understanding of the tax system. Given that many will in fact go into a small business for themselves, the problem becomes an issue for society.

The are many self-help books available. My recommendation is to read as much as possible, as these will give you a different slant of wealth creation. This book will also help you form the foundation of being financially successful.

But don't stop here. The tools mentioned in this book are only some of the tools you need to create a life of abundance for yourself and your family. Remember the aeroplane safety message: 'Fit your own oxygen mask first so you can help others.' Become wealthy so you can be a valuable member of society and help those less fortunate than you.

Some of this information may seem extremely basic. I never cease to be amazed at how little some business owners know about these areas. Yes, they are good at what they do, being a plumber, electrician or computer programmer, but when it comes to business and tax skills, they have never been exposed to it at the level discussed in the book.

Getting your mindset right is about many things. It starts with being fixated about creating wealth by building an asset base to generate passive income. Forsake certain spending habits that are not aligned with this goal, like always having a new car, nights out with friends, using credit cards and spending your future income on things that do not hold their value. Be careful about what you read, particularly in the mainstream press, about the next new trend. Don't listen to the wrong people; take charge of your own destiny to set goals that are lifetime strategies. Forsake short-term gains for long-term wealth creation tactics.

It is something I have been doing for over 40 years, every day. For a business owner, it is something they may do once a month or once a year.

You need to apply the lessons listed. I have provided you with the things you need to know.

Property is a long game. Don't expect any 'get rich quick' purchases. Sometimes they happen, but that is rare. Remember the rule of compounding. Compounding works extremely well if you hold a property for a long period of time. The rule of 72 tells you how long it takes an asset to double in value. For example, if the average increase is 7 per cent, it will take a property 10 years to double in value (72 divided by 7 = 10.3 years).

In your lifetime, you will go through a number of property cycles. You must ride them out. Be aware that time will always fix any initial mistakes, so do not be quick to sell.

Mindset is about getting your purpose right. Decide what will drive you. What are your inner reasons for embarking on this journey? This is often referred to as your prime purpose (prime being similar to a prime number [1, 3, 5, 7, etc], which cannot be divided into other numbers). Define a purpose that is true to your aims and ambitions and not capable of being sidetracked. Start by asking yourself two simple questions:

1. What is it that, when you are doing it, time has no meaning? When you have total focus? Something you are genuinely passionate about it, that gives you that spring in your step?

2. When you are doing something, is it something that you seem to be good at? You find it easy and yet others tell you how great you are? Doors seem to open easily?

Now, from the above, write a mission statement for yourself. I know many think of mission statements as applying to businesses, but I want you to think of your personal life path like a business. Write something that is true to you. It could be something like:

- 'I want to be in control of my life both financially and physically.'
- 'I want to move to a position where my time is spent only doing what I want to do.'
- 'I want to provide for myself, my family and those that I love, so that they never endure any financial hardship.'

Once you have an idea of your 'why', you will know why you are investing in property: the boundaries, the trade-offs and when enough is enough. You will know when it is time to say, 'I have the assets to satisfy my personal mission statement and I intend to utilise the assets and the income I have created.'

As the saying, goes there is more to life than financial wealth. Wealth creates opportunities but, more importantly, it creates the freedom to do whatever you want to do. That must be the end goal of any wealth creation strategy.

## 34

# The ripple effect

Those reading this book will come from many different backgrounds and experiences. I feel that the one thing readers of this book will share will be a thirst for knowledge. The biggest barrier to knowledge is thinking you know it all. If you think you know it all, then you will not be open to learning new things.

One of my favourite quotes about communication is by Mark Twain. It goes, 'If God intended us to talk more than listen, he would have given us two mouths and one ear.' Listening is so important to communication. Learning new things, being humble enough not to think you know it all. We all know that change is the only certainty in life. Nothing ever remains the same. Property is no exception to this.

What has this got to do with building a retirement nest egg that will mean you will never be dependent on others for a living? It is simply this: only a small proportion of the population will listen, learn and take steps to financial freedom. Only a few will save every cent they can to get onto the first rung of the (self-sufficient) ladder. Others will make excuses as to why they can't do it, be distracted or listen to the wrong people that have a negative view about creating wealth. They will say it can't be done. But the truth is that many have done exactly the steps in the book, so this argument is incorrect. If you aspire to be in this small elite group of self-sufficient investors, you need to rise above the masses and be a leader. Be a quiet leader that others will look up to.

What is the ripple effect? When you throw a stone into the water, the water ripples outward from that stone. You, as a leader, need to be that stone, entering an environment (a business, community, family) that sends small waves outwards to others. In business, this happens when the right CEO comes into a business and takes it to new heights. They don't do it alone, but lead by example and make their team sing to the same tune. Have you ever wondered how a CEO could be worth, say, $10.4 million in wages (eg the CBA CEO)? But if they take the share price from $100 per share to $150.00, take the company's profit from $4 billion to $9.8 billion, then surely, they are worth it.

You, as the reader of this book, have a challenge. Can you achieve the same for yourself, your family, your society and those around you? Can you create a ripple effect to contribute back to society a legacy that you now have the means to do? Can you produce this effect for all of those around you, such that you will lead by this example?

Can you take the first steps to financial freedom, no matter what excuses may come your way, or what age you are? Do you have the courage?

# Acknowledgements

Pat Mesiti – For the marketing and content ideas, and for convincing me that I have a story that needed to be told.

Corinna Essa – For assisting me with the first edition of this book to get the content right and the marketing plans.

Mark Anastasi – For his enlightening book and ideas on the millionaire mindset, and for allowing me to reproduce some of those ideas.

In researching the material for this book, I have reviewed the websites of the Australian Taxation Office, Chartered Accountants Australia and New Zealand and CPA Australia. Some of the content in this book is a result of that research and some of the material, being of a public nature, has been reproduced or paraphrased for this book.